# THE COMFORT FOOD

COOK BOOK

# THE COMFORT FOOD COOK BOOK

**CAROLINE BRETHERTON, NICHOLA FLETCHER, SOPHIE GRIGSON, and HEATHER WHINNEY**

London, New York, Melbourne,
Munich, and Delhi

**Photography** Deepak Aggarwal, Peter Anderson,
Angela Coppola, Tim de Neefe, William Reavell,
Julie Renouf, William Shaw, Stuart West

**Editors** Lucy Bannell, Emma Callery, Michael Fullalove,
Sophie Grigson (soups), Kathy Steer
**Project Editors** Robert Sharman, Alison Shaw, Shashwati Tia Sarkar
**Designers** Sara Robin, John Round, Kathryn Wilding, Jade Wheaton
**Managing Editor** Dawn Henderson
**Managing Art Editor** Christine Keilty
**Creative Technical Support** Sonia Charbonnier

**Editor** Cécile Landau
**Jacket Designer** Mark Penfound
**Artworkers** David McDonald, Kavita Varma
**Indexer** Hilary Bird
**Producer** Stacey McDermott

This edition produced for The Book People,
Hall Wood Avenue, Haydock, St. Helens WA11 9UL

Published in Great Britain in 2013
by Dorling Kindersley Limited
80 Strand, London WC2R 0RL
Penguin Group (UK)

Contains content from *The Soup Book* (2009),
*The Slow Cook Book* (2011), *Sausage* (2012)
and *The Pie Book* (2013)

10 9 8 7 6 5 4 3 2 1
001–192908–Jan/13

Copyright © 2013 Dorling Kindersley Ltd

ISBN 978-1-4093-2791-2

Colour reproduction by Colourscan, Singapore
Printed and bound in China by South China Printing Co. Ltd

Discover more at
**www.dk.com**

# Contents

# soups

The cornerstone of many soups is a well-made stock and, though the ingredients for it may seem humble and the preparation simple, the contribution it makes is vital.

# Making stock

The four stocks most commonly called for in soup-making are chicken stock, brown stock, fish stock, and vegetable stock. Made from bones and/or common vegetables and flavourings, they are easy to prepare and freeze well for up to three months. If produced from meat bones, stock is clear and relatively fat-free, though it will be gelatinous enough to set when cold. Vegetable stock is lighter and requires a careful balance of ingredients to make it flavoursome. Stocks should not be seasoned with salt – they are one of the building blocks for a soup, not a dish in their own right.

## selection of stocks

**brown stock** is so called because it is produced from meat bones that have been "browned" by cooking in fat. It jellies when cold.

**vegetable stock** can be given extra depth by the addition of mushrooms, potato, and tomatoes that will offset the sweetness of the other veg.

**fish stock** is quick to make, ideally from the bones and heads of salmon or mild-flavoured white fish, especially flat fish like sole and plaice.

**chicken stock** serves as the base for many a fine soup. Some raw or cooked chicken bones and a few standard aromatics are all that's required to produce a rich, gelatinous stock.

This recipe gives an ideal list of ingredients, but as long as you have the chicken carcase, onion, carrot, and one or two of the herbs, you can turn out a fine stock.

# Chicken stock

1 raw or cooked chicken carcase,
    roughly broken into pieces
1 onion, quartered
1 carrot, quartered
1 leek, quartered
1 celery stalk, quartered

1 bay leaf
2 parsley stalks
a sprig of thyme
8 black peppercorns
1.7 litres (3 pints) cold water

**1** Put the chicken, vegetables, and all the flavourings into a large pan, cover with the water, and bring to the boil. Cover with a lid, lower the heat, and simmer for 2–3 hours, skimming off any foam from time to time.

**2** Ladle the stock through a sieve into a clean bowl, pressing the ingredients firmly against the sides of the sieve with the back of the ladle to squeeze out as much liquid as possible.

**MAKES** 1.5 L (2¾ PINTS)    **PREP** 5 MINS **COOK** 3 HOURS    **FREEZE** 3 MONTHS

**3** If you're using the stock straightaway, remove any globules of fat from the surface by skimming the top of the stock with a piece of kitchen paper folded in two.

**4** Otherwise, leave the stock to cool before chilling it in a covered container for up to 3 days. A layer of congealed fat will form on the surface. Scoop this off before use.

### microwave chicken stock

If you are short of time, you can also make chicken stock in a microwave. Put the broken-up chicken carcase into a large microwaveable bowl along with the onion, carrot, leek, and celery. Add the bay leaf, parsley, thyme, and peppercorns, then cover with boiling water. Cover the bowl with cling film (roll it back at one edge to allow the steam to escape) and microwave on full power for 25 minutes. Leave to stand for a further 25 minutes, then strain.

For a rich meat-based stock, use either beef or lamb bones, but never a mixture of the two. If you have any bacon rinds or vegetable trimmings to hand, pop them in the pot too.

# Brown stock

1.35kg (3lb) raw or cooked beef
  or lamb bones
2–3 onions, halved
2–3 carrots, halved

a bouquet garni (see p127)
2.5–3 litres (4½–5¼ pints)
  cold water
1 tsp black peppercorns

**1** If you're using raw bones, roast them with the onions and carrots in an oven preheated to 200°C (400°F/Gas 6), turning them frequently, for 30 minutes or until browned. If you're using cooked bones, start the stock from step 2.

**2** Put all the ingredients into a large pan, bring to the boil, then skim off any foam that rises to the surface with a slotted spoon. Lower the heat, cover with a lid, and simmer for 3–4 hours. Strain the stock through a sieve, pressing the ingredients against the sides of the sieve to extract all the liquid. Leave to cool, then chill in a covered container for up to 3 days. Before use, remove any solidified fat from the surface with a slotted spoon, then bring the stock to the boil.

**hale and hearty**
A meaty stock based on beef or lamb makes a world of difference to hearty broth-based soups like French onion soup.

**MAKES** 2.5 L (4¼ PINTS)  **PREP** 10 MINS **COOK** 3½–4½ HOURS  **FREEZE** 3 MONTHS

This is an excellent stock, with a good balance of flavours. The potato means it will not be clear, but since it is being used in a soup, that doesn't matter.

# Vegetable stock

1 leek, thickly sliced
1 large carrot, thickly sliced
2 celery stalks, thickly sliced
1 onion, roughly chopped
75g (2½oz) button, chestnut, or open-cup mushrooms, quartered

1 medium potato, thickly sliced
1 tomato, quartered
3 parsley stalks
2 bay leaves
4 sprigs thyme
1.5 litres (2¾ pints) cold water

**1** Put all the ingredients into a large pan. Bring to the boil, then lower the heat, cover with a lid, and simmer very gently for 30 minutes.

**2** Strain the stock through a fine sieve, pressing the ingredients well against the sides of the sieve to extract all the liquid. Leave to cool completely, then chill in a covered container for up to 3 days before use.

**light and fragrant**
A flavoursome vegetable stock makes a good alternative to chicken stock, whether you are vegetarian or not.

🌑 **MAKES** 1 L (1¾ PINTS)   🕐 **PREP** 5 MINS **COOK** 35 MINS   ❄ **FREEZE** 3 MONTHS

Ask the fishmonger for the bones when getting fish filleted, and check if they have any extra that they can give you. Fish bones will freeze, well-wrapped, for up to two months.

# Fish stock

675g–1kg (1½–2¼lb) salmon or white fish
   bones, heads, and skin (don't use those
   from dark, oily fish such as mackerel,
   herring, and sardines – they will give
   the stock an unpleasant flavour)
6 black peppercorns
1 sprig of thyme

1 bay leaf
2 parsley stalks
2 small carrots
1 onion
2 celery stalks
1 generous glass of dry white wine
1.7 litres (3 pints) cold water

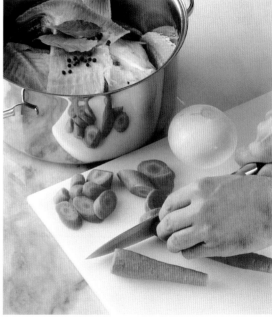

**1** Put the fish heads and bones into a large pan, breaking or cutting them up with a knife to fit. Add the black peppercorns, thyme, bay leaf, and parsley.

**2** Roughly chop the vegetables and add to the pot with the wine. Place the pan over a moderate heat and let the wine bubble for 3 minutes. Add the water and bring to the boil.

⊙ **MAKES** 1.5 L (2¾ PINTS)   🕐 **PREP** 5 MINS **COOK** 30 MINS   ❄ **FREEZE** 2 MONTHS

**3** Lower the heat and simmer, uncovered, for 20–25 minutes – no longer or the stock may begin to develop a bitter taste. Skim off any scum from time to time with a slotted spoon.

**4** Strain the stock through a fine sieve into a bowl, pressing the solids against the side of the sieve to extract all the liquid. Leave to cool completely, then chill in a covered container for up to 3 days.

**5** The finished stock should be thin in texture, with a delicate flavour. It will make an excellent base for all kinds of fish soup.

Among the easiest soups to prepare are those you whiz to a purée in a blender. The alternative is to use a food mill – this requires a little more effort, but the results are smoother.

# Puréeing

The secret to success with puréed soups is thorough cooking, so that the starchy ingredients that give the soup its body can be blended to a smooth purée. For that reason, always cook root vegetables and dried beans till they are extremely tender, but never overcook potatoes, or they will become glutinous and gluey. There is also a range of semi-puréed soups, in which some of the ingredients are blended to thicken the broth, while the rest are left whole for interest.

### in a blender

**1** Before blending, test the ingredients are really tender with a knife – they are only ready to purée when completely soft.

**2** Blend the soup until you have a smooth consistency with no lumps. Do it in batches so you don't overload the machine.

**3** The consistency of a puréed soup will vary according to the ingredients used and the way in which they're processed. But, in general, it should be totally smooth and lump-free. To remove all traces of skins, seeds, and fibres, you may need to push the purée through a fine sieve.

## using a food mill

Working the ingredients through a food mill is particularly successful for soups that contain ingredients with skins and seeds, which blenders sometimes can't cope with.

## semi-pureed soups

To thicken a soup but keep some texture for interest, purée around half of it and then return it to the pan. Gently reheat the soup before serving.

A little butter or cream stirred into a soup just before serving will enrich it (see pp22–3), but there will be times when you want to thicken a soup rather more. Here's how to do it.

# Thickening

There are several quick and easy ways you can give body to a soup at the end of cooking. You could whisk egg yolk or a mixture of egg yolk and cream into the hot liquid. Another option is to use starch, in the form of cornflour, plain flour, or rice flour. Or you could make a paste from flour and butter and stir this into the soup before serving. But perhaps the oldest method of thickening a soup is with bread, either stirred into the broth at the last minute or incorporated into it earlier in the cooking process.

## with starch

Mix a little cornflour, rice flour, or plain flour to a thin paste with some cold water. Stir the mixture into the pan of hot soup, bring back to the boil, and simmer, stirring all the time, for 1–2 minutes or until the soup thickens.

## with flour and butter

Combine two parts softened butter to one part flour. Gradually whisk small pieces of the paste into the hot soup at the end of cooking. Allow the flour to cook for 1–2 minutes, stirring all the time.

## with egg

Added towards the end of cooking, egg yolk or a mixture of egg yolk and cream will thicken a hot soup and make it velvety. Remove the pan from the heat to incorporate the mixture, then reheat the soup gently, whisking until thick. Do not allow it to boil or it will curdle.

## with bread

Bread has long been used to thicken country soups. For gazpacho (left), breadcrumbs are blended into the soup at an early stage. But bread can also be added to a broth at the last minute, and stirred until it breaks up and thickens the soup.

Butter or cream stirred into a soup at the last minute will greatly improve its character, adding body and shine. For interest, you can flavour the butter and serve it at the table.

# Enriching

Both cream and butter make a quick and simple garnish for individual servings of soup (see p26–7), but if you have another garnish in mind, you can add them to the soup to enrich it while it's still in the pan. Butters flavoured with herbs, nuts, or smoked fish are another way of enriching a soup, although these are best served separately, to be added to the soup by your guests.

## with cream

## with butter

Add the cream at the end of cooking and, in the case of a puréed soup, after blending. Stir it in well, then check the seasoning. If you've added a substantial amount, you may want to reheat the soup gently before serving.

Cut a knob of chilled unsalted butter into cubes. Remove the pan from the heat and whisk it in a cube at a time – the soup should become glossy and smooth. Do not reheat the soup or the butter will separate.

## with a flavoured butter

Flavoured butters are an ideal accompaniment to puréed soups and bisques. They are also easy to prepare and work well with a variety of ingredients. Blend the flavourings of your choice into the butter, then place the butter on a sheet of greaseproof paper and roll it tightly into a cylindrical shape. Chill it in the fridge or freezer until you're ready to dish up the soup, then simply slice it into rounds. You could also serve the butter at the table and allow your guests to help themselves. Here are recipes for two flavoured butters that are great with a whole range of soups.

## herb butter

Mix 60g (2oz) softened butter with 6 blanched and finely chopped spinach leaves, 1 chopped shallot, 1 tsp each chopped parsley, chervil, and tarragon, and some salt and pepper. Roll in greaseproof paper and chill till needed.

## lemon and chilli butter

Combine 60g (2oz) softened butter with 1 tsp finely grated lemon zest and ¼ tsp crushed dried chilli flakes (or more if you like your food quite spicy). Season to taste with salt.

There's no need to worry if your soup hasn't turned out quite as you had intended – even the most accomplished cook occasionally produces a dish that's less than perfect.

# Rescuing

Whether you are unhappy with the finished consistency or think the soup is too highly seasoned, here are some quick fixes to put things right.

### too thin

There are a number of ways you can thicken a soup that's too thin. You could whisk in a paste of butter and flour or a mixture of eggs and cream (as here). Or you could add some rice flour, cornflour, or plain flour blended with water (for more details, turn to pp20–1). Another option is to stir in a few instant potato flakes or a little instant oat cereal.

### too thick

Depending on the liquid you've used to produce the soup, thin it with a little stock, milk, or water. Once the soup has reached the desired consistency, taste it, season, and reheat gently.

## stringy or lumpy

Even a soup you've whizzed in a blender can turn out lumpy or stringy. Ladle it into a fine sieve, then use the back of the ladle, a wooden spoon, or a pestle to push the ingredients through. Reheat gently before serving.

## too salty

If you only ever add salt towards the end of cooking and use home-made stock that's unseasoned, the chances of your soup being too salty are slim. But if it is, there are a couple of things you can do. Add a couple of raw potatoes cut in half and simmer the soup gently until they're cooked, then remove and discard. Alternatively, add a little sugar and, if the soup is also too thick, some cream, milk, or water.

From a single piece of seafood to a simple swirl of cream, a well chosen garnish transforms a soup, adding extra colour, as well as texture and flavour.

# Garnishing

For some soups, a garnish is an essential component – the soured cream stirred into Borscht, for instance, or the cheese-topped croûtes served with French onion soup. For others, a garnish is a way of introducing contrasting textures and flavours. Many ingredients can act as a garnish if they also complement the flavour of the soup, but here is a selection to suit almost every occasion.

**with cream** Dolloped, swirled, or drizzled, cream makes an excellent garnish for thick puréed soups. Use single cream, double cream, whipped cream, soured cream, or crème fraîche. Yogurt is an alternative if you're counting the calories.

**with shellfish** A whole prawn, crab claw, grilled scallop, or (as here) an oyster poached and served in its shell makes a spectacular garnish for a seafood soup. A wild garlic flower provides the finishing touch or this dish.

**with herbs** Fresh sage leaves or parsley fried in olive oil until crisp make a flavoursome garnish for gutsy soups, but a sprinkling of chopped parsley, chervil, or coriander instantly adds fragrance and colour to almost any soup.

**with vegetables** Raw or cooked, vegetables make eye-catching and healthy garnishes. If small, like peas, they can be served whole therwise, slice them into decorative strips, dice, or rings.

**with croûtons** Small dice of fried bread are a classic garnish. For about 40 croûtons, cut 4 slices of day-old white bread (crusts removed) into 1cm (½in) dice. Heat 2 tbsp sunflower oil and 30g (1oz) unsalted butter in a large frying pan until hot, then fry the dice, stirring constantly, for 10 minutes or until golden. Drain on kitchen paper before serving. For extra flavour, stir in a finely chopped garlic clove a couple of minutes before the croûtons are due to be done.

**with bacon** Grilled until crisp and then crumbled, bacon makes a tasty garnish that looks attractive floating on the surface of a pale puréed soup. Here it is accompanied by pieces of pan-fried scallop.

**with seeds or nuts** Toasted seeds or nuts not only look pretty, they also lend a satisfying crunch. Served with a vegetable soup, they are a good source of protein too.

**with croûtes** Large croûtons are known as croûtes. To make them, cut a day-old baguette into 1cm (½in) slices, and toast until golden. Alternatively, place on a baking sheet and bake in an oven preheated to 180°C (350°F/Gas 4) for 15 minutes.

Pushing this colourful, zingy soup through a sieve may seem fiddly, but it does wonders for the texture and is worth the effort.

# Carrot cream with onion and cumin

2 tbsp sunflower, groundnut or mild olive oil
2 large Spanish onions, peeled
  and coarsely chopped
1 tsp cumin seeds
1 tsp ground cumin
1kg (2¼lb) carrots, peeled and
  coarsely chopped

sea salt and freshly ground black pepper
juice and grated zest of 1 small
  unwaxed orange
120ml (4fl oz) single cream
1 tbsp finely chopped flat-leaf parsley

**1** Place a large sauté pan over a medium-high heat. Add the oil and tip in the onion and cumin. Cook for 3–5 minutes, or until softened, stirring frequently. Add the carrots and 1.5 litres (2¾ pints) water, then season lightly. Bring to a simmer, reduce the heat, cover and cook for 20 minutes, or until the carrots are very tender. Turn off the heat and allow to cool a little.

**2** Pour into a blender or food processor and whiz until smooth. Place a sieve over a saucepan (or the sauté pan if possible). Pour the soup into the sieve and push it through with the back of a wooden spoon.

**3** Taste and adjust the seasoning. Stir in the orange juice and zest. Reheat until piping hot and stir in the cream, then the parsley. Season with a little extra pepper. Serve hot.

**SERVES** 4      **PREP** 20 MINS **COOK** 30 MINS      **FREEZE** UP TO 3 MONTHS,
BEFORE CREAM IS ADDED

This thickly textured, satisfying soup is a Russian classic
to enjoy at any time of year and on any occasion. Try it with
grated carrot piled on top and hunks of dark rye bread.

# Borscht

45g (1½ oz) butter or goose fat
2 large beetroot, roughly grated
1 onion, roughly grated
1 carrot, roughly grated
1 celery stalk, roughly grated
400g can chopped tomatoes
1 garlic clove, crushed (optional)
1.7 litres (3 pints) hot vegetable stock
2 bay leaves
4 cloves
2 tbsp lemon juice
salt and freshly ground black pepper
200ml (7fl oz) soured cream

**1** Melt the butter in a large saucepan over a medium heat. Add the beetroot, onion, carrot, and celery, and cook, stirring, for 5 minutes or until just softened. Add the tomatoes and garlic, if using, and cook for 2–3 minutes, stirring frequently, then stir in the stock.

**2** Tie the bay leaves and cloves in a small piece of muslin and add to the pan. Bring the soup to the boil, then lower the heat, cover, and simmer for 1 hour 20 minutes. Discard the muslin bag, stir in the lemon juice, and season to taste with salt and pepper. Ladle the soup into warm bowls and add a swirl of soured cream to each one.

**SERVES** 4     **PREP** 15 MINS **COOK** 1½ HOURS     **FREEZE** UP TO 3 MONTHS

This soup should be sharp, sweet, and spiced – the juice of a whole lemon, one or two tablespoons of sugar, and quite a generous seasoning of salt and pepper are recommended.

# Beet and apple soup

1 onion, halved
2 garlic cloves
3 tbsp olive oil
salt and freshly ground black pepper
350g (12oz) raw beetroot, peeled and halved
1 potato, halved
4 eating apples, peeled and cored
1.5 litres (2¾ pints) hot vegetable stock
  or chicken stock

1–2 tbsp dark brown sugar
juice of 1 lemon
2 tbsp finely chopped parsley, chives,
  dill, or coriander, or a mixture
200g (7oz) crème fraîche, soured cream,
  or thick creamy yogurt

**1** Grate the onion and garlic in a food processor. Heat the oil in a large pan over a low heat, add the onion, garlic, and a pinch of salt, and cook gently, stirring once or twice, for 5 minutes or until soft. Meanwhile, grate the beetroot, potato, and apples in the food processor.

**2** Add the beetroot, potato, and apples to the pan and stew gently for 10 minutes, stirring occasionally. Pour in the stock, bring to the boil, then cover with a lid and simmer gently for 45 minutes or until the beetroot is cooked through.

**3** Transfer the mixture to a blender and whiz till smooth. You may need to do this in batches. Season with the sugar, lemon juice, and some salt and freshly ground black pepper.

**4** Stir the chopped herbs into the cream or yoghurt, then ladle the soup into warm bowls and drop a big spoonful of green-speckled cream into the middle of the deep pink soup.

**SERVES** 6–8    **PREP** 20 MINS **COOK** 1 HOUR    **FREEZE** UP TO 3 MONTHS
WITHOUT THE HERB CREAM

This rustic soup owes its substance to haricot beans. Buy fresh beans when they are available in early summer – they are quicker to cook and easier to digest.

# Pistou soup

### For the pistou
3 garlic cloves, smashed and peeled
coarse sea salt to taste
leaves from a large handful of fresh basil
2 small tomatoes, skinned, seeds removed and chopped (see p123)
freshly ground black pepper
25g (scant 1oz) Parmesan cheese, grated
3 tbsp olive oil

1 ham hock, or a thick piece of smoked bacon, about 150g (5½ oz)

200g (7oz) fresh white haricot beans, such as cannellini, shelled
100g (3½oz) fresh red haricot beans, such as borlotti, shelled
250g (9oz) flat green beans, sliced
2 medium floury potatoes, diced
3 tomatoes, skinned, seeds removed and chopped (see p123)
4 medium courgettes, chopped
salt and freshly ground black pepper
100g (3½oz) small macaroni

**1** To make the pistou, pound the garlic in a mortar with a pestle, then add a little salt and the basil and pound to a paste. Add the tomatoes and continue pounding and mixing until you have a thick sauce. Add pepper, the cheese, and the oil, mix well, and adjust the seasoning.

**2** For the soup, put 2 litres (3½ pints) cold water in a large stewing pot. Add the ham hock. Bring to a simmer, then partly cover and leave to bubble gently for 30 minutes, skimming occasionally.

**3** Meanwhile, put the haricot beans in a saucepan, cover with plenty of cold water, and bring to the boil. Simmer for 10 minutes, drain and refresh. Add all the vegetables to the stewing pot. Season lightly. Return to a simmer, then part-cover and bubble gently for 1 hour, skimming occasionally.

**4** Remove the ham hock and shred the meat. Lift half of the ingredients out of the pan, mash with a fork, then return to the soup with the ham. Add the macaroni and cook until just tender. Stir in the pistou, and serve.

**SERVES** 6–8    **PREP** 30 MINS **COOK** 1½ HOURS    **FREEZE** UP TO 3 MONTHS
WITHOUT THE PISTOU

This soup is a perfect spring starter. Try serving it topped with a splash of extra virgin olive oil and cubes of bread fried in olive oil.

# Baby broad bean soup

3 slices toasting bread, for croûtons
6 tbsp olive oil
3 large mild onions, sliced
1 leek, sliced
1.5kg (3lb 3oz) broad beans, shelled

4 garlic cloves, crushed
a small handful of fresh chives, chopped
4 new potatoes, peeled and chopped
salt and freshly ground black pepper
leaves from a bunch of fresh radishes

**1** To make the croûtons, cut the bread into 1.5cm (½in) cubes. Heat 3 tbsp oil in a large frying pan over a fairly hot heat. Add the bread cubes and spread them out. Fry for a minute, then stir and turn them over. Fry for another minute. Spread the croûtons over a plate lined with kitchen paper. Pat with more kitchen paper to drain off excess oil. Set aside.

**2** In a big stewing pot or flameproof casserole, heat the remaining oil over a moderate heat. Add the onions and leek. Soften for 10 minutes, stirring frequently.

**3** Add the broad beans to the pot with the garlic, chives, and potatoes. Stir, then pour in about 3 litres (5¼ pints) water. Season lightly and stir in the radish leaves. Turn up the heat a little and bring to the boil, then leave to bubble gently for 15–20 minutes.

**4** Allow to cool a little, then work through a food mill. Alternatively, whiz briefly in a blender, then press through a sieve. (If you prefer, you can omit the sieving, in which case the soup will serve 6–8 people.) Reheat until piping hot before serving, topped with the croûtons.

**SERVES** 4–6     **PREP** 20 MINS **COOK** 1 HOUR     **FREEZE** UP TO 3 MONTHS
WITHOUT THE CROÛTONS

If you have grown your own sweetcorn, wait until the very last minute to harvest it – the quicker you get it from the plot to the pan, the sweeter it will be.

# Sweetcorn chowder

4 fresh corn on the cob
500ml (16fl oz) water
salt
2 bay leaves
2 tbsp olive oil
1 large onion, chopped
4 fresh sage leaves, chopped, or
  ½ tsp dried sage, crushed
1 tsp fresh thyme leaves, or
  ½ tsp dried thyme

1 medium carrot, chopped
2 celery sticks, chopped
1 large potato, chopped
200g (7oz) cream cheese
120ml (4fl oz) milk
salt and freshly ground black pepper
single cream, to serve
dusting of paprika, to serve

**1** Stand each corn cob upright in a large bowl and strip the kernels by cutting downward with a sharp knife. Set the kernels aside. Place the cobs in a large saucepan and add water, a generous dose of salt, and bay leaves. Bring to the boil and simmer, covered, for 15 minutes. Remove and discard the cobs and bay leaves.

**2** Heat the oil in a saucepan and cook the onions until translucent. Add the herbs and remaining vegetables except the corn kernels. Cook for about 5 minutes, until softened. Add the corn cob stock and simmer until the potato is collapsing. Meanwhile, place the sweetcorn kernels in a saucepan and barely cover with cold water. Bring to the boil and cook for 2 minutes. Set aside.

**3** Add the cream cheese and milk to the soup mixture, then purée until smooth. Stir in the corn kernels with their cooking liquid. Give the chowder one more whiz if desired, to break up the corn kernels slightly. Reheat and adjust the seasoning. Ladle into warm bowls. Drizzle with streaks of single cream and dust with paprika.

⊘ **SERVES** 4–6    ⏱ **PREP** 10 MINS **COOK** 30 MINS     ❄ **FREEZE** UP TO 1 MONTH
WITHOUT MILK OR CREAM CHEESE

Try this hearty soup with slices of dark German rye bread and a glass of white wine or wheat beer. Warming and perfect for a wintry day.

# Pea and sausage soup

30g (1oz) butter
1 large carrot, peeled and diced
1 small leek, diced
2 stalks celery, diced
1 medium potato, peeled and diced
½ bunch fresh parsley, chopped
125ml (4fl oz) dry white wine
1.2 litres (2 pints) hot chicken stock
3 Toulouse sausages
750g (1lb 10oz) peas (frozen or fresh)
salt and pepper

**1** Preheat the oven to 180°C (350°F/Gas 4). In a large saucepan, melt the butter and add the carrot, leek, celery and potato and cook, stirring, until softened. Add the parsley, wine and stock and simmer for 15 minutes.

**2** Place the sausages on a baking tray and cook, turning occasionally, for 15–20 minutes, or until cooked through and golden brown on all sides, then slice and set aside.

**3** Add the peas to the pot and cook for 3–4 minutes, or until just al dente. Season and process to a puree in a blender. Return to the pot and heat through. Serve in 6 bowls, garnished with the sliced cooked sausage.

**SERVES** 6    **PREP** 20 MINS **COOK** 20 MINS    **FREEZE** UP TO 3 MONTHS
WITHOUT THE SAUSAGES

This easy and delicious supper or light lunch dish showcases the spiciness of chorizo. Make sure you use the best chorizo you can find. If you like, you can make a double batch of this soup, and freeze half for another day.

# Tomato and chorizo soup

2 tbsp olive oil
250g (9oz) chorizo, in small cubes
2 red onions, finely chopped
4 celery sticks, finely chopped
4 carrots, finely chopped
3 garlic cloves, grated
   or finely chopped
salt and freshly ground black pepper
700g jar passata
1.2 litres (2 pints) hot vegetable stock
2 x 400g cans chickpeas,
   drained and rinsed
handful of fresh coriander,
   finely chopped, to serve

**1** Heat half the oil in a large, heavy saucepan. Add the chorizo, and cook over a medium heat, stirring occasionally, for 5 minutes, or until it begins to turn crispy. Remove and set aside.

**2** Heat the remaining oil in the pan, add the onions, and cook over a low heat for 6–8 minutes, or until soft and translucent. Stir in the celery, carrots, and garlic, and season with salt and pepper. Cook over a low heat, stirring occasionally, for 8 minutes, or until tender.

**3** Add the passata, stock, and chickpeas, and simmer for 15 minutes. Return the chorizo to the pan, then taste and season again if needed. Stir through the coriander, and serve.

**SERVES** 8 **PREP** 20 MINS **COOK** 40 MINS **FREEZE** UP TO 3 MONTHS

This extra-special version of the old standard – using fresh, sun-dried, and roasted tomatoes, takes the humble tomato to new heights.

# Cream of tomato soup

50g (1¾oz) butter
1 tbsp olive oil
2 onions, finely chopped
2 celery sticks, finely chopped
2 carrots, finely diced
2 garlic cloves, minced
12 plum tomatoes, about 1kg (2¼lb), quartered, roasted, and roughly chopped

8 plum tomatoes, about 600–720g (1¼–1½lb), skinned and finely chopped (see p123)
6 sun-dried tomatoes, finely chopped
1 litre (1¾ pints) hot vegetable stock
2–3 tbsp double cream
salt and freshly ground black pepper

**1** Heat the butter and olive oil in a heavy saucepan over a medium heat. Add the onions, and sauté for 8–10 minutes, stirring frequently, until very soft but not coloured. Next, add the celery and carrots, and continue cooking gently without burning for another 10 minutes, stirring from time to time. Add the garlic and sauté for another 2 minutes, stirring.

**2** Mix together the roasted plum tomatoes, fresh tomatoes, and sun-dried tomatoes. Tip into the pan with any juices, and cook, stirring, for 5 minutes to allow the flavours to combine; if the sauce looks too thick or starts catching on the bottom of the pan, add a little of the hot vegetable stock. Pour in the remaining vegetable stock, and simmer the soup for 15–20 minutes.

**3** Blend the soup to a smooth purée using a food processor or hand-held blender. Pass through a sieve or mouli into a clean pan, unless you prefer to make a peasant-style soup. Add the double cream a teaspoon at a time until you are happy with the taste and texture. Season with salt and pepper, reheat very gently if needed, and serve.

**SERVES** 4–6     **PREP** 30 MINS **COOK** 40 MINS     **FREEZE** UP TO 3 MONTHS
BEFORE THE CREAM IS ADDED

In Russia and the Ukraine, borscht often includes tomatoes as well as beetroot. This version may seem unusual, but you will love its rich colour and fantastic taste.

# Tomato borscht

2 tbsp olive oil
1 small onion, finely chopped
1 garlic clove, chopped
225g (8oz) raw beetroot, peeled
   and finely grated
1 tsp freshly ground toasted cumin seeds
¼ tsp ground cinnamon
225g (8oz) ripe fresh tomatoes,
   skinned and roughly chopped

250ml (8fl oz) tomato juice
1 tbsp sun-dried tomatoes,
   very finely chopped
600ml (1 pint) vegetable stock
1 tbsp light soy sauce
salt and freshly ground black pepper
toasted cumin seeds, to serve
soured cream or crème fraîche, to serve

**1** Heat the oil in a heavy pan over a low heat. Gently cook the onion and garlic for about 5 minutes, then add the beetroot. Sweat gently for a further 10 minutes, stirring from time to time, until softened but not browned.

**2** Add the ground spices, tomatoes, tomato juice, and sun-dried tomatoes, then pour in the stock. Bring to the boil. Reduce the heat slightly, cover, and simmer very gently for 15 minutes or until all the vegetables are soft. Remove from the heat. Blend or process until velvety smooth. Check the seasoning, adding the soy sauce, salt, and pepper to taste.

**3** Serve chilled, at room temperature, or slightly warm. If you do reheat the soup, do so gently over a low heat. To serve, spoon into serving bowls, and garnish with toasted cumin seeds and a spoonful of soured cream or crème fraîche.

**SERVES** 6–8      **PREP** 20 MINS **COOK** 1 HOUR      **FREEZE** UP TO 3 MONTHS
WITHOUT THE HERB CREAM

Fresh lime juice, coriander, and dried poblano chillies –
not to mention the corn tortillas – give a Mexican flavour
to this spicy tomato soup.

# Sopa de tortilla

5 tbsp sunflower oil
½ onion, finely chopped
2 large garlic cloves, finely chopped
450g (1lb) tomatoes, skinned
1.5 litres (2¾ pints) chicken stock
   or vegetable stock
1 or 2 dried poblano chillies, deseeded

2 soft corn tortillas, cut into strips
3 tbsp chopped fresh coriander
2 tbsp fresh lime juice
salt and freshly ground black pepper
85g (3oz) Gruyère cheese, grated
2 limes, cut into wedges, to serve

**1** Heat 1 tbsp of the oil in a large saucepan over a medium heat. Add the onion and fry, stirring, for 5 minutes, or until softened. Add the garlic and stir for 30 seconds. Using a blender, whiz with the tomatoes until smooth.

**2** Tip the tomato-onion purée into the pan and simmer for 8–10 minutes, stirring constantly. Stir in the stock and bring to the boil. Reduce the heat, partially cover the pan, and simmer for 15 minutes, or until thickened.

**3** Place a non-stick frying pan over a medium heat. Add the chillies and press them against the pan with a spatula until they blister. Turn them over and repeat. Remove from the pan, cut into small pieces, and set aside.

**4** Heat the remaining oil in the frying pan until sizzling hot. Add the tortilla strips in batches and fry until just crisp. Remove with a slotted spoon and drain on kitchen paper.

**5** When ready to serve, add the chillies to the soup, bring to the boil and simmer for 3 minutes, or until the chillies are soft. Stir in the coriander and lime juice, and season with salt and pepper to taste. Divide the toasted tortilla strips between 4 soup bowls. Ladle in the soup and top with a sprinkling of cheese. Serve with wedges of lime.

**SERVES** 4          **PREP** 15 MINS **COOK** 50 MINS          **FREEZE** UP TO 3 MONTHS
                                                                AT THE END OF STEP 3

The last-minute addition of paprika-flavoured chorizo gives spice to this hearty soup. Keep the texture chunky by processing only briefly.

# Fennel soup with beans, thyme, and chorizo

250g (9oz) dried haricot beans
1 tbsp sunflower, groundnut or mild olive oil
1 Spanish onion, finely chopped
2 cloves garlic, crushed
1 head fennel, cored and finely chopped
2 tsp dried fennel seeds
1 tbsp finely chopped fresh parsley
2 tsp thyme leaves
salt and pepper
100g (3½oz) diced cubed chorizo

**1** Soak the beans overnight in plenty of cold water then drain and rinse. Put a heavy pan over a medium heat. Add the oil, spread in the onion and stir for 2 minutes. Add the garlic, fennel and fennel seeds, parsley and half the thyme and cook for 3–5 minutes until slightly softened. Tip in the beans. Stir, pour in 2 litres (3½ pints) water and season lightly.

**2** Bring to a simmer and cook for 40 minutes, or until the beans are tender, skimming from time to time. Remove from the heat and leave to cool a little. Transfer to a food processor or blender and whiz briefly until partly puréed. Return to the pan, taste and adjust the seasoning.

**3** Gently reheat the soup. Meanwhile, place a small non-stick pan over a moderately high heat and fry the chorizo for 2–3 minutes until crisp and coloured, stirring frequently. Drain on a plate lined with kitchen paper.

**4** Ladle the soup into bowls, add a little chorizo to each and finish with a scattering of thyme. Serve immediately.

**SERVES** 4      **PREP** 15 MINS PLUS SOAKING OVERNIGHT      **FREEZE** UP TO 3 MONTHS
**COOK** 1 HOUR      WITHOUT CHORIZO

A very simple soup, easy to make and with very few ingredients, this is lifted out of the ordinary by the gentle aniseed tang of dill.

# Courgette and potato soup

2 large potatoes, peeled and diced
500ml (16fl oz) hot chicken stock
1 tsp salt
1 tbsp olive oil
3 medium courgettes, peeled,
    finely diced or grated
1 onion, peeled, finely diced or grated
white pepper
100ml (3½fl oz) double cream
300ml (10fl oz) milk
small bunch of fresh dill, chopped

**1** Place the potatoes into a large pan with the hot stock and salt, bring to the boil and simmer for about 5 minutes, or until tender. Blend with a stick blender until smooth and return to the saucepan.

**2** In another saucepan, heat the olive oil, add the courgettes and onion and fry over a gentle heat for 2–3 minutes or until slightly softened but not coloured. Stir in a dash of the pepper, the cream, milk and puréed potato broth and simmer gently for 5 minutes, or until the courgettes have softened. Add dill and season to taste. Serve hot.

**SERVES** 4    **PREP** 10 MINS **COOK** 15 MINS    **FREEZE** UP TO 3 MONTHS

This soup is just as good in summer made with fresh tomatoes and basil pesto stirred through it, as it is in winter with added canned beans to bulk it out. It is excellent for freezing.

# Provençal vegetable soup

1 tbsp olive oil
1 onion, finely chopped
salt and freshly ground black pepper
3 garlic cloves, finely chopped
2 celery sticks, finely chopped
2 carrots, peeled and roughly chopped
sprig of tarragon, leaves finely chopped
2 sprigs of rosemary
400g can tomatoes, blended until smooth

900ml (1½ pints) hot vegetable stock, for both methods
3 potatoes, peeled and chopped into bite-sized pieces
325g (11oz) green dwarf beans or French or fine green beans, trimmed and chopped into bite-sized pieces
30g (1oz) Parmesan cheese, grated (optional)

**1** Heat the oil in a large heavy-based pan over a medium heat, add the onion, and cook for 3–4 minutes until soft. Season with salt and pepper, then stir through the garlic and celery and cook for a further 5 minutes or until the celery is soft.

**2** Stir in the carrots, tarragon, and rosemary and cook for a minute, then tip in the puréed tomatoes and a little stock, and bring to the boil. Add the remaining stock and return to the boil, then reduce to a simmer, partially cover with the lid, and cook gently for about 45 minutes. If more liquid is needed, top up with a little hot water. Add the potatoes for the last 15 minutes of cooking.

**3** When the potatoes are soft, add the beans and cook for a further 10 minutes, or until they are cooked but retain a bite. Taste and season, remove the rosemary, and ladle into warmed large shallow bowls. Sprinkle over the Parmesan, if using, and serve with some crusty French bread.

**SERVES** 4-6    **PREP** 15 MINS **COOK** 1 HOUR    **FREEZE** UP TO 3 MONTHS

Make this soup near the end of the summer when tomatoes and peppers are plentiful. It freezes well and is also a cheering stalwart for winter meals.

# Roasted red pepper, fennel and tomato soup

1 large fennel bulb, peeled
1 red onion
2 red peppers, halved and deseeded
500g (1lb) tomatoes
4 garlic cloves, in their skins
1.5 tsp sugar
2 tbsp olive oil
1 large sprig of fresh rosemary, leaves only

1–2 tbsp vegetable oil
1.5 tsp fennel seeds
½ tsp nigella seeds
400ml (14fl oz) passata
1 litre (2 pints) vegetable stock
1 red chilli, split and deseeded
salt and freshly ground black pepper
handful of fennel leaves

**1** Preheat the oven to 200°C (400°F/Gas 6). Cut the fennel and onion into wedges. Slice a cross into the base of each tomato and squeeze the juice and seeds into a bowl. Strain the juice and set aside.

**2** Line a roasting tin with baking parchment and add the fennel, onion, peppers, tomatoes, and garlic cloves. Sprinkle over the sugar, drizzle with the olive oil, and scatter the rosemary on top. Roast the vegetables for about 1 hour, until the tomatoes are soft. Cool the vegetables before peeling the blackened skin from the peppers. Peel the garlic and discard the skins.

**3** Heat the vegetable oil in a large pan and toss in the fennel and nigella seeds, swirling them around for a few seconds. Pour over the passata, the stock and the reserved tomato juice, and bring to the boil. Add the roasted vegetables, pop the chilli into the pan and season with salt and pepper to taste. Half cover with a lid and simmer for about 45 minutes.

**4** Using a blender, whiz the soup until smooth and press through a sieve. Reheat, re-season, and finish with a sprinkling of fennel leaves.

**SERVES** 4-6   **PREP** 25 MINS **COOK** 2 HOURS   **FREEZE** UP TO 3 MONTHS

Mounded together in the centre of the bowl, the vegetables in this soup resemble coins – which is one of the reasons it got its name. The other is that it is very inexpensive to make.

# "Penny" soup

1 leek
300g (11oz) potatoes
250g (9oz) large carrots
175g (6oz) small sweet potatoes
1 tbsp olive oil
15g (½oz) butter
600ml (1 pint) hot vegetable stock
1 tbsp chopped flat-leaf parsley
salt and freshly ground black pepper

**1** Slice the vegetables into 3mm (⅛in) rounds. Heat the oil and butter in a large saucepan, add the leeks, and cook over a medium heat, stirring frequently, for 3–4 minutes or until soft. Add the potatoes, carrots, and sweet potatoes and cook, stirring, for 1 minute.

**2** Pour in the stock, then bring to the boil, cover with a lid, and simmer for 20 minutes or until the vegetables are tender but not soft. Transfer about one-third of the vegetables to a blender or food processor with a little of the liquid and blend to a smooth purée, then return to the pan. Stir in the parsley, season to taste with salt and freshly ground black pepper, and serve, with the vegetables in a little mound in the centre.

**SERVES** 4      **PREP** 15 MINS **COOK** 30 MINS      **FREEZE** UP TO 3 MONTHS
WITH ALL VEGETABLES PUREED

Use whatever proportion of carrots and Jerusalem artichokes you have, adding up to 700g (1lb 9oz) in total. The carrots enhance the colour and sweetness of the soup.

# Jerusalem artichoke soup with saffron and thyme

2 tbsp virgin rapeseed oil or olive oil,
    plus extra to garnish
2 medium onions, chopped
3 garlic cloves, chopped
350g (12oz) Jerusalem artichokes,
    scrubbed and roughly chopped
350g (12oz) carrots, scrubbed and
    roughly chopped
sea salt and freshly ground black pepper
1.2 litres (2 pints) hot vegetable stock
1 tbsp fresh thyme leaves or
    1½ tsp dried thyme
large pinch (about 30 strands)
    of saffron
juice of ½ lemon

**1** Heat the oil in a large pan over a medium heat, add the onions, and fry for 5–10 minutes or until soft and translucent. Add the garlic and fry for 30 seconds or until fragrant. Stir in the artichokes, carrots, and a little salt, then cover with a lid and sweat, stirring frequently, for 10–15 minutes or until the vegetables are softened.

**2** Add the stock, thyme, and saffron, bring to the boil, then lower the heat to a simmer and cook for 20 minutes or until the vegetables are thoroughly soft. Cool briefly, then whiz until smooth in a blender. Stir in the lemon juice and season to taste with salt and freshly ground black pepper. Serve in warm bowls, with a drizzle more oil on top.

SERVES 4-6    PREP 15 MINS **COOK** 30-45 MINS    FREEZE UP TO 3 MONTHS

A fantastic way to use this much maligned, fragrant weed –
choose young and tender specimens and wear a double layer
of latex gloves to pick them.

# Nettle soup

2 tbsp virgin rapeseed oil or olive oil
4 spring onions or 1 bunch, sliced
3 leeks, roughly chopped
650g (1lb 7oz) potatoes, washed but not
    peeled, cut into 2cm (¾in) cubes
sea salt
1 litre (1¾ pints) vegetable stock
100g (3½oz) young nettles or nettle tips
    (about ¼ carrier bag full), washed
juice of half a lemon
freshly ground black pepper
plain thick yogurt, to serve

**1** Heat the oil in a soup pan over a medium heat. Add the spring onions, leeks and
potatoes with a little sea salt. Stir, cover, and cook for 5 minutes, stirring frequently.

**2** Add the stock and bring to the boil. Add the nettles, stir, and simmer for 10 minutes,
or until the potato is soft. Cool briefly, then purée using a hand blender or food processor
until completely smooth. Taste for seasoning, then squeeze in a little lemon juice and grind
in some pepper. Serve each bowl with a dollop of thick yogurt and more pepper.

**SERVES** 4     **PREP** 10 MINS **COOK** 20 MINS     **FREEZE** UP TO 3 MONTHS

Simple, affordable, and immensely satisfying, this hearty soup makes a warming meal when accompanied with some freshly baked crusty bread.

# Cream of vegetable soup

45g (1½oz) butter
2 carrots, sliced
1 leek (white part only), sliced
2 parsnips, sliced
1 onion, sliced
1 small turnip, sliced
3 celery stalks, sliced
1 potato, sliced

1.2 litres (2 pints) hot vegetable stock
2 tsp fresh thyme leaves
1 bay leaf
pinch of grated nutmeg
salt and freshly ground black pepper
3 tbsp single cream
3 tbsp milk
bunch of chives, snipped, to garnish

**1** Melt the butter in a large pan, add the carrots, leek, parsnips, onion, turnip, celery, and potato, and stir to coat well. Cover the pan with a lid and cook for 10–15 minutes or until the vegetables have softened.

**2** Add the stock, thyme, bay leaf, and nutmeg, then season with salt and freshly ground black pepper. Bring to the boil and simmer, uncovered, for 30–40 minutes or until the vegetables are meltingly soft. Scoop out the bay leaf and discard.

**3** Whiz the soup in a blender until smooth. You may need to do this in batches. If you like the texture of your soups very smooth, strain it through a fine sieve, otherwise leave it as it is. Stir in the cream and milk, adding more milk if the consistency is still too thick. Season with salt and freshly ground black pepper, then reheat gently. Garnish with the chives and serve.

**SERVES** 6 **PREP** 15 MINS **COOK** 40-55 MINS **FREEZE** UP TO 3 MONTHS
WITHOUT THE CREAM AND MILK

This Parisian classic is given extra punch with a spoonful of brandy in every bowl. Serve it the moment you've made it – French onion soup must be piping hot.

# French onion soup

30g (1oz) butter
1 tbsp sunflower oil
675g (1½lb) onions, thinly sliced
1 tsp sugar
salt and freshly ground black pepper
120ml (4fl oz) red wine
2 tbsp plain flour
1.5 litres (2¾ pints) hot beef stock
4 tbsp brandy
8 croûtes (see p27)
1 garlic clove, cut in half
115g (4oz) Gruyère or Emmental, grated

**1** Melt the butter with the oil in a large, heavy pan over a low heat. Add the onions and sugar and turn to coat well. Season with salt and freshly ground black pepper, then press a piece of damp greaseproof paper on top of the onions. Cook, uncovered, stirring occasionally, for 40 minutes or until they are a rich dark brown colour. Take care not to let them stick and burn.

**2** Remove the greaseproof paper and stir in the wine. Increase the heat to medium and stir for 5 minutes while the onions glaze. Sprinkle in the flour and stir for 2 minutes, then pour in the stock and bring to the boil. Reduce the heat to low, cover with a lid, and leave to simmer for 30 minutes. Taste and season with salt and freshly ground black pepper, if necessary.

**3** Preheat the grill to its highest setting. Divide the soup among flameproof bowls and stir 1 tbsp of the brandy into each. Rub the croûtes with the cut garlic and place one in each bowl. Sprinkle with the cheese and grill for 2–3 minutes or until the cheese is bubbling and golden. Serve at once.

**SERVES** 4    **PREP** 10 MINS **COOK** 1HOUR 20 MINS    **FREEZE** UP TO 1 MONTH
WITHOUT THE CROUTES AND CHEESE

Meltingly soft onions make a flavoursome base for this lightly spiced soup enriched with almonds and sweetened with a hint of caramel.

# Onion and almond soup

1 onion, very finely sliced
½ tsp sea salt flakes
vegetable oil, to deep-fry
100g (3½oz) almonds (with skins on)
750ml (1¼ pints) hot chicken stock
60g (2oz) butter
¼ tsp nigella seeds

4 large onions, diced
1 red chilli, chopped
1 tsp muscovado sugar
2 tbsp balsamic vinegar
120ml (4fl oz) single cream
salt and freshly ground black pepper

**1** For a fried onion garnish, put the onion slices in a shallow dish, sprinkle with the sea salt, then set to one side for at least 2 hours. Using your hands, squeeze out the liquid, then pat dry with kitchen paper. Deep-fry in hot oil for 1–2 minutes or until golden, then drain on kitchen paper.

**2** Bring a small pan of water to the boil, add the almonds, turn off the heat, and cover with a lid. Leave to soak for 15 minutes, then drain and slip off the skins once the nuts are cool enough to handle. Transfer to a food processor with 100ml (3½fl oz) of the stock, then whiz to a paste and set aside.

**3** Meanwhile, melt the butter in a large pan, add the nigella seeds, and fry over a gentle heat for 1 minute. Stir in the diced onions and chilli, cover, and cook over a very low heat for 20–30 minutes or until soft but not brown, then turn up the heat and remove the lid. When the onions begin to turn a golden colour, stir in the sugar, and cook until it starts catching on the bottom of the pan. Add the vinegar and continue cooking until sticky.

**4** Add the rest of the stock and the almond paste and simmer for 20 minutes. Whiz the soup until smooth in a blender, then return to the pan, stir in the cream, and season with salt and freshly ground black pepper. Reheat gently and serve garnished with the fried onions.

**SERVES** 4 　　　**PREP** 20 MINS, PLUS 2 HOURS SALTING **COOK** 1 HOUR 　　　**FREEZE** UP TO 2 MONTHS BEFORE CREAM IS ADDED

Using a selection of both wild and cultivated mushrooms produces a soup bursting with flavour. The horseradish cream provides a welcome kick.

# Mushroom soup

30g (1oz) butter
1 onion, finely chopped
2 celery sticks, finely chopped
1 garlic clove, crushed
450g (1lb) mixed mushrooms,
   roughly chopped
200g (7oz) potatoes, peeled and cubed
1 litre (1¾ pints) vegetable stock
2 tbsp finely chopped fresh parsley
salt and freshly ground black pepper
horseradish cream, to serve (optional)

**1** Melt the butter in a large saucepan, add the onion, celery, and garlic,  and fry for 3–4 minutes, or until softened.

**2** Stir in the mushrooms and continue to fry for a further 5–6 minutes. Add the potatoes and the stock, and bring to the boil. Reduce the heat and leave to simmer gently for 30 minutes.

**3** Using a blender, whiz the soup until smooth, working in batches if necessary. Sprinkle over the parsley and season to taste with salt and pepper. Serve immediately, stirring a little horseradish cream into each soup bowl, if desired, for an extra kick.

**SERVES** 4     **PREP** 10 MINS **COOK** 45 MINS     **FREEZE** UP TO 3 MONTHS

Robust, garlicky, and fragrant with rosemary and sage, this is a hearty, satisfying soup. Serve it with some fresh crusty bread and a drizzle of good-quality olive oil.

# Bean and rosemary soup

2 tbsp olive oil
2 onions, finely chopped
salt and freshly ground black pepper
1 tbsp finely chopped fresh rosemary leaves
a few fresh sage leaves, finely chopped
4 celery stalks, finely chopped
3 garlic cloves, grated or finely chopped
2 tbsp tomato purée
2 x 400g cans borlotti beans, drained,
    rinsed, and drained again
1.2 litres (2 pints) hot chicken stock
2.5kg (5½lb) potatoes, cut into
    chunky pieces

**1** Heat the oil in a large pan, add the onions, and cook over a low heat for 6–8 minutes or until soft and translucent. Season well with salt and freshly ground black pepper, then stir in the rosemary, sage, celery, and garlic and cook over a very low heat, stirring occasionally, for 10 minutes.

**2** Stir in the tomato purée and beans and cook gently for 5 minutes. Pour in the stock, bring to the boil, then add the potatoes and simmer gently for 15 minutes or until cooked. Taste, season with salt and freshly ground black pepper, if needed, and serve.

**SERVES** 8     **PREP** 15 MINS **COOK** 40 MINS     **FREEZE** UP TO 3 MONTHS

Be careful when seasoning this hearty soup, as the bacon means that little, if any, extra salt will be needed. Try this dish with olive oil croûtons.

# Split pea and bacon soup

250g (9oz) dried split green peas, rinsed
and drained
1.5 litres (2¾ pints) water
250g (9oz) piece smoked streaky bacon
¼ celeriac, peeled and diced
1 large carrot, diced
1 small leek, diced
1 medium floury potato, peeled and diced
1tsp dried marjoram
15g (½oz) butter
1 onion, diced
freshly ground black pepper
3–4 tsp chopped chives, to garnish

**1** Put the peas in a large saucepan with the water and bring to the boil. Add the bacon, cover, and cook for about 40 minutes over a medium heat. Add the celeriac, carrot, leek, and potato, and stir in the marjoram. Bring to the boil again, cover, and cook for another 20 minutes.

**2** Melt the butter in a pan, and add the onion. Brown slightly, stirring continuously, then set aside.

**3** Remove the bacon from the soup. Discard the excess fat and rind. Shred the meat and return it to the soup together with the fried onion. Season it with pepper. Sprinkle with chopped chives to serve.

**SERVES** 6　　**PREP** 30 MINS **COOK** 1 HOUR 10 MINS　　**FREEZE** UP TO 3 MONTHS

This hearty, substantial soup improves with reheating, so it benefits from being made a day in advance. Reheat gently over a low heat.

# Tuscan bean soup

4 tbsp extra virgin olive oil, plus
  extra for drizzling
1 onion, chopped
2 carrots, sliced
1 leek, sliced
2 garlic cloves, chopped
400g (14oz) can chopped tomatoes
1 tbsp tomato purée
900ml (1¾ pints) chicken stock

salt and freshly ground black pepper
400g (14oz) can borlotti beans,
  flageolet beans, or cannellini beans,
  drained and rinsed
250g (9oz) baby spinach leaves
  or spring greens, shredded
8 slices ciabatta bread
grated Parmesan cheese, for sprinkling

**1** Heat the oil in a large saucepan and fry the onion, carrot, and leek over a low heat for 10 minutes, or until softened but not coloured. Add the garlic and fry for 1 minute. Add the tomatoes, tomato purée, and stock. Season to taste with salt and pepper.

**2** Mash half the beans with a fork and add to the pan. Bring to the boil, then lower the heat and simmer for 30 minutes. Add the remaining beans and spinach to the pan. Simmer for a further 30 minutes.

**3** Toast the bread until golden, place 2 pieces in each soup bowl, and drizzle with olive oil. To serve, spoon the soup into the bowls, top with a sprinkling of Parmesan, and drizzle with a little more olive oil.

**SERVES** 4    **PREP** 15 MINS **COOK** 1 HOUR 20 MINS    **FREEZE** UP TO 3 MONTHS
AT THE END OF STEP 2

This hearty, wholesome soup takes the edge off chilly winter weather. It's worth using dried beans, which have a much fuller flavour than the canned variety.

# Creamy kidney bean soup

225g (8oz) dried kidney beans,
   soaked overnight in cold water
2 red onions, diced
400g can chopped tomatoes
1 tbsp tomato purée
5 garlic cloves, halved
5cm (2in) fresh root ginger, roughly chopped
3 large green chillies
salt and freshly ground black pepper
150ml (5fl oz) single cream
squeeze of fresh lime juice, to taste

**For the garnish**
1 small mouli, coarsely grated, or
   4–6 red radishes, sliced
1 large green chilli, finely chopped
2 tbsp chopped fresh coriander leaves
squeeze of fresh lime juice, to taste

**1** Drain the kidney beans, discarding the soaking liquid. Put the beans in a very large heavy-bottomed pan and cover with 1.7 litres (3 pints) of water. Add the onions, tomatoes, tomato purée, garlic, ginger, and chillies.

**2** Cover the pan and simmer for about 3 hours, until the beans are just breaking up. Top up the liquid if required during cooking. Alternatively, use a pressure cooker – the beans will be tender in about 30 minutes.

**3** Once the beans have cooled slightly, scoop out the chillies. Using a blender, whiz the soup until smooth in batches, then sieve to remove the skins. Season well with salt and pepper, stir in the cream and reheat. Add lime juice to taste.

**4** For the garnish, combine the grated mouli or sliced radish with the green chilli and coriander leaves. Sharpen with a squeeze of lime, then top each bowl of soup with a small heap of the herby mouli.

 **SERVES** 6     **PREP** 20 MINS **COOK** 3¼ HOURS
      OR 40 MINS IN A PRESSURE COOKER

   **FREEZE** UP TO 3 MONTHS
AT THE END OF STEP 3

This thick soup from northern Italy is guaranteed to keep out the winter chills. Soak the beans overnight to rehydrate them and cut down on the cooking time.

# White bean soup

3 tbsp olive oil
2 onions, finely chopped
2 garlic cloves, crushed
225g (8oz) dried cannellini beans, soaked overnight
1 celery stick, chopped
1 bay leaf
3–4 parsley stalks, without leaves
1 tbsp lemon juice

1.2 litres (2 pints) vegetable stock
salt and freshly ground black pepper
3 shallots, thinly sliced
60g (2oz) pancetta, chopped (optional)
85g (3oz) Fontina cheese or Taleggio cheese, chopped into small pieces

**1** Heat 2 tbsp olive oil in a saucepan, add the onions, and fry over a low heat for 10 minutes, or until softened, stirring occasionally. Add the garlic and cook, stirring, for 1 minute.

**2** Drain the soaked beans and add to the pan with the celery, bay leaf, parsley stalks, lemon juice, and stock. Bring to the boil, cover, and simmer for 1½ hours, or until the beans are soft, stirring occasionally.

**3** Remove the bay leaf and liquidize the soup in batches in a blender, or through a hand mill. Rinse out the pan. Return the soup to the pan and season to taste with salt and pepper.

**4** Heat the remaining olive oil in a small frying pan, and fry the shallots and pancetta (if using) until golden and crisp, stirring frequently to stop them sticking to the pan. Reheat the soup, adding a little stock or water if it is too thick. Stir the Fontina into the soup. Ladle into individual bowls, and sprinkle each serving with the shallots and pancetta.

**SERVES** 4     **PREP** 30 MINS **COOK** 2 HOURS     **FREEZE** UP TO 3 MONTHS
AT THE END OF STEP 3

This hearty vegetarian soup has just a touch of spice and is quick and easy to prepare. Serve with plain, low-fat yogurt and good crusty bread.

# Lentil soup

1 tbsp olive oil
2 onions, finely chopped
2 celery sticks, finely chopped
2 carrots, finely chopped
2 garlic cloves, crushed
1–2 tsp curry powder
150g (5½oz) red lentils
1.4 litres (2½ pints) vegetable stock
120ml (4fl oz) tomato juice or vegetable juice
salt and freshly ground black pepper

**1** Heat the oil in a large pan over a medium heat, then add the onions, celery, and carrots. Cook, stirring, for 5 minutes, or until the onions are soft and translucent.

**2** Add the garlic and curry powder and cook, stirring, for a further 1 minute, then add the lentils, stock, and tomato juice.

**3** Bring to the boil, then lower the heat, cover, and simmer for 25 minutes, or until the vegetables are tender. Season to taste with salt and pepper, and serve hot.

**SERVES** 4 **PREP** 20 MINS **COOK** 35 MINS **FREEZE** UP TO 3 MONTHS

This chunky country soup takes minutes to prepare and makes a good supper or lunch dish. For a vegetarian option, leave out the lardons.

# French cabbage soup

1 tbsp olive oil
100g (3½oz) small lardons, or diced bacon
1 Spanish onion, finely chopped
1 garlic clove, crushed
1 large Savoy cabbage, halved, core
   discarded, and leaves cut into shreds
sea salt and freshly ground black pepper
3 sprigs parsley
croûtons (see p27), to garnish (optional)

**1** Heat the oil in a large heavy casserole over a medium heat. Add the lardons (setting aside 2 tbsp to finish), onion, and garlic. Fry, stirring frequently, for 3–4 minutes or until the onion and garlic start to colour. Add the cabbage shreds, reserving a handful to finish. Stir well and season lightly with sea salt and generously with pepper. Continue frying for 2–3 minutes, stirring occasionally.

**2** Bring about 850ml (about 1½ pints) water to the boil in a kettle. Pour the boiling water over the vegetables and lardons, stir well, and add the parsley. Cover, lower the heat a little, and simmer gently for about 20 minutes, stirring occasionally.

**3** Meanwhile, place a non-stick frying pan over a medium heat. Add the reserved lardons and fry until crisp and golden. Then add the reserved cabbage shreds and fry them until they have wilted, stirring frequently. Season with a little pepper.

**4** Taste the soup and adjust the seasoning. Lift out the parsley. Ladle into individual bowls and scatter over the fried bacon and cabbage mixture. A few croûtons scattered across the surface provide a nice finishing touch.

**SERVES** 4     **PREP** 15 MINS **COOK** 30 MINS     **FREEZE** UP TO 3 MONTHS
WITHOUT THE LARDON GARNISH

Cauliflower is transformed when treated to gentle heat and aromatic spicing. For a vegetarian option, garnish this with croûtons and Parmesan cheese instead of bacon.

# Cauliflower soup with toasted coriander

2 tsp coriander seeds
40g (1½oz) unsalted butter
1 onion, diced
1 potato, diced
1 head cauliflower, finely chopped
500ml (16fl oz) vegetable stock

1 bay leaf
8 streaky bacon rashers, rinds removed
200ml (7fl oz) milk
100ml (3½fl oz) single cream
salt and freshly ground black pepper

**1** Heat a sturdy frying pan or small griddle and lightly roast the coriander seeds, stirring all the time, for about a minute. Grind the seeds to a coarse powder using a mortar and pestle and set aside.

**2** Melt the butter in a large saucepan over a low heat. Add the onion and potato, cover and leave to soften for 10 minutes. Add the cauliflower and ground coriander, season well, cover and continue cooking for a further 10 minutes.

**3** Pour over the stock, add the bay leaf, cover, and simmer for about 15 minutes, until the cauliflower has softened. Meanwhile, cook the bacon rashers under a hot grill until crisp. Drain on kitchen paper, roughly chop, and set aside.

**4** Remove the bay leaf and blend the soup to a purée with a stick blender or in a liquidizer. Stir in the milk and add the cream. Reheat and season again if necessary. Ladle the soup into bowls and scatter with the chopped bacon before serving.

**SERVES** 4–6     **PREP** 15–20 MINS **COOK** 40 MINS          **FREEZE** UP TO 1 MONTH
WITHOUT CREAM OR BACON

This is a substantial meal-in-one that is full of complex flavours. It's also one of those dishes that tastes better when reheated, so if you have the time, make it a day ahead and reheat to eat.

# Moroccan harira soup

1 tbsp olive oil
1 red onion, finely chopped
salt and freshly ground black pepper
3 garlic cloves, finely chopped
1 celery stick, chopped
675g (1½lb) shoulder or shank of lamb, cut into bite-sized pieces
1 tsp ground turmeric
1 tsp ground cinnamon
5cm (2in) piece of fresh root ginger, peeled and finely chopped

900ml (1½ pints) hot vegetable stock for the slow cooker (1.4 litres/2½ pints for the traditional method)
125g (4½oz) green or brown lentils, rinsed well and picked over for any stones
400g can chickpeas, drained and rinsed
1 tsp harissa paste
few sprigs of coriander, leaves only, to serve

**1** Heat the oil in a large flameproof casserole over a medium heat, add the onion, and cook for 3–4 minutes until soft. Season with salt and pepper, then stir through the garlic and celery and cook for a further 6–10 minutes until the celery is soft.

**2** Add the lamb, turmeric, cinnamon, and ginger. Increase the heat a little, stir until the lamb is coated, and cook for 6–10 minutes until the lamb is no longer pink. Add a ladleful of stock and bring to the boil. Stir through the lentils and chickpeas, turning them to coat evenly, add the remaining stock, and bring back to the boil.

**3** Reduce to a gentle simmer and cook for 1–1½ hours until the lamb is meltingly tender. Check occasionally that it's not drying out, topping up with a little hot water if needed. Stir through the harissa paste and cook for a few more minutes. Ladle into warmed bowls, top with coriander leaves, and serve with lemon wedges on the side.

SERVES 4–6    PREP 25 MINS **COOK** 2 HOURS    FREEZE UP TO 1 MONTH

As delicate as it is delicious, this pretty, pastel-green soup is scented with citrussy cardamom notes, which make a marvellous marriage with the pounded pistachios.

# Creamy pistachio soup

125g (4½oz) (shelled weight) unsalted
  pistachio nuts
1 green chilli, cut in half and deseeded
120ml (4fl oz) hot water
6 green cardamom pods, crushed and
  seeds extracted
1 small blade of mace
½ tsp coriander seeds, dry-roasted (see p127)
25g (scant 1oz) butter
2 large garlic cloves, finely chopped

small bunch of spring onions (white
  parts only), finely chopped
2.5cm (1in) piece of root ginger, peeled
  and finely chopped
½ tsp garam masala
450ml (15fl oz) hot vegetable stock
100ml (3½fl oz) single cream
1 tbsp chopped coriander leaves
salt and freshly ground black pepper

**1** Bring a pan of water to the boil, add the pistachios, and cook for 2–3 minutes. Drain in a colander and refresh under cold running water. Pat the nuts dry with kitchen paper, then turn out on to a tea towel. Give them a vigorous rub with the towel – the skins should slip off easily. Reserve a generous tablespoon for garnishing and put the rest in a food processor. Add the chilli and hot water and process to a rough paste, then set aside.

**2** Grind the cardamom seeds, mace, and coriander to a powder with a pestle and mortar. Melt the butter in a saucepan over a medium heat, add the garlic, spring onions, and ginger, and soften for 2–3 minutes. Stir in the ground spices and garam masala and cook for a few seconds, then add the pistachio paste and stock. Simmer, without a lid, for 10–15 minutes, stirring occasionally.

**3** Blend in batches until smooth. Stir in the cream and coriander leaves, then season with salt and freshly ground black pepper. Serve the soup garnished with the reserved pistachio nuts roughly chopped.

**SERVES** 2–3    **PREP** 40 MINS **COOK** 20 MINS    **FREEZE** UP TO 2 MONTHS
WITHOUT CREAM AND CORIANDER

Originally nothing more than a humble fisherman's soup using the remains of the day's catch, bouillabaisse has evolved into one of the great Provençal dishes.

# Bouillabaisse

4 tbsp olive oil
1 onion, thinly sliced
2 leeks, thinly sliced
1 small fennel bulb, thinly sliced
2–3 garlic cloves, finely chopped
4 tomatoes, skinned, deseeded, and chopped
1 tbsp tomato purée
250ml (8fl oz) dry white wine
1.5 litres (2¾ pints) fish stock or chicken stock
pinch of saffron threads
strip of orange zest
1 bouquet garni
salt and freshly ground black pepper

2 tbsp Pernod
1.35kg (3lb) mixed white and oily fish and shellfish, such as gurnard, John Dory, monkfish, red mullet, prawns, and mussels, heads and bones removed
8 croûtes (see p27), to serve

**For the rouille**
125g (4¼oz) mayonnaise
1 bird's-eye chilli, deseeded and roughly chopped
4 garlic cloves, roughly chopped
1 tbsp tomato purée
½ tsp salt

**1** Heat the oil in a large pan over a medium heat. Add the onion, leeks, fennel, and garlic and fry, stirring, for 5–8 minutes, or until the vegetables are soft but not coloured. Stir in the tomatoes, tomato purée, and wine.

**2** Add the stock, saffron, zest and bouquet garni. Season with salt and pepper, and bring to the boil. Reduce the heat, partially cover, and simmer for 30 minutes, stirring occasionally. Whiz the rouille ingredients in a blender until smooth. Transfer to a bowl, cover, and chill until required.

**3** Just before the liquid finishes simmering, cut the fish into chunks. Remove the zest and bouquet garni and add the firm fish. Reduce the heat to low and simmer for 5 minutes. Add the delicate fish and simmer for 2–3 minutes, or until it is cooked through and flakes easily. Stir in the Pernod and season to taste. To serve, spread the croûtes with rouille and place 2 in the bottom of each bowl. Ladle the soup on top.

**SERVES** 4      **PREP** 20 MINS **COOK** 45 MINS

This flavourful soup needs no accompaniment, but croûtes rubbed with garlic, spread with rouille (see p80), or topped with Gruyère cheese are a welcome addition.

# Soupe de poissons

5 tbsp olive oil
4 medium onions, chopped
2 leeks, chopped
1.5–2kg (3lb 3oz–4½lb) mixed
   fish and seafood
4 pieces dried fennel stalks,
   5cm (2in) long
4 medium, ripe tomatoes, quartered

9 garlic cloves, crushed
5 sprigs of fresh flat-leaf parsley
3 bay leaves
15cm (6in) strip dried orange peel
1 tbsp tomato purée
salt and freshly ground black pepper
pinch of saffron threads
6 croûtes (see p27), to serve

**1** Put the oil in a large, heavy saucepan. Add the onions and leeks, and soften over a moderate heat until just golden.

**2** Gut the larger fish. Rinse all the fish and seafood. Add to the pan and stir, then add the fennel, tomatoes, garlic, parsley, bay leaves, orange peel, and tomato purée. Stir and cook for 8–10 minutes until the fish is just beginning to flake when pierced with a fork. Pour in 2.5 litres (4 pints) hot water and season lightly with salt and pepper. Reduce the heat and simmer gently for 20 minutes.

**3** Remove from the heat. Leave to cool a little, stirring and mashing down the soft fish pieces with the back of a large wooden spoon. Remove the fennel, orange peel, and bay leaves. If you like, whiz the soup to a rough purée in a blender. Push the soup through a chinois or a very fine sieve into a clean saucepan. Return the soup to a simmer over a moderate heat.

**4** Soften the saffron in a ladleful of the soup, then stir into the rest of the soup in the pan. Adjust the seasoning. Ladle the soup into bowls. Serve hot, with croûtes.

**SERVES** 6      **PREP** 20 MINS **COOK** 1 HOUR      **FREEZE** UP TO 2 MONTHS

This soup from Brittany was originally a way to use the leftover catch of the day. Try it with haddock, smoked haddock, pollock or cod.

# Cotriade

2 large floury potatoes, peeled
2 tbsp groundnut, sunflower or mild olive oil
30g (1oz) butter
2 Spanish onions, coarsely chopped
1 litre (1¾ pints) light fish stock
3 sprigs of thyme
3 bay leaves
3 sprigs of flat-leaf parsley
sea salt and freshly ground black pepper
800g (1¾lb) mixed fish, skinned, cut into
    large chunks
4 thick slices country bread, to serve

**For the dressing**
5–6 tbsp groundnut, sunflower
    or mild olive oil
½ tsp Dijon mustard
sea salt and freshly ground black pepper
1 tbsp white wine or cider vinegar
2 tbsp finely chopped parsley

**1** Cut the potatoes in half then cut each half into four and set aside. Put the oil and butter in a large, heavy sauté pan. Add the onions and soften over a moderate heat until just golden, stirring frequently. Add the stock then tip in the potatoes and herbs. Season lightly, stir, cover and cook for 12–15 minutes or until the potatoes are almost cooked.

**2** Place the fish in the pan and season lightly. Gently stir then cook for 10 minutes, or until the fish just starts to flake when pierced with a fork. If you are freezing this soup, cool and do so now. Meanwhile, make the dressing. In a cup or small jug, mix together the oil and mustard and season, then whisk in the vinegar until emulsified. Stir in the parsley.

**3** Remove the soup from the heat and adjust the seasoning. Lift out the herbs. Put the bread in 4 warm bowls and moisten with a little dressing. Ladle over the soup and drizzle on the remaining dressing. Serve hot.

**SERVES** 4     **PREP** 20 MINS **COOK** 30 MINS

Replace the mussels with shell-on prawns in this Flemish soup if you prefer; peel, and add the empty shells to the reduced stock for 3 minutes before straining.

# Waterzooi

1 large waxy potato, peeled
1 large carrot, peeled
1 medium-large courgette
400g (14oz) asparagus
300g (10oz) monkfish
1 sole, filleted and skinned
600ml (1 pint) light chicken or fish stock

100ml (3½fl oz) dry white wine
3 large spring onions, finely chopped
500g (1lb 2oz) mussels, rinsed and scrubbed
100ml (3½fl oz) whipping cream
salt and pepper
1 tbsp finely chopped tarragon, to serve

**1** Cut the potato and carrot in 1 x 5cm (½ x 2in) batons. Slice the courgette on the diagonal. Cut off the asparagus tips, then chop the spears into 5cm (2in) lengths. Cut the monkfish into 4cm (1½in) chunks and cut each sole fillet crossways in half. Set the vegetables and fish aside separately.

**2** Put the stock, wine and spring onions (reserving a few to serve) in a casserole dish. Bring to the boil over a moderate heat. Add the potato, reduce the heat to a simmer and cook for 5 minutes, then add the carrot and cook for 5 minutes. Add the courgette and asparagus and cook for 1–2 minutes, or until all is al dente. Lift out the vegetables and set aside.

**3** Bring the stock to the boil over a high heat and reduce by a third. Reduce the heat to a simmer, tip in the mussels, cover and cook for 3–4 minutes. Strain through a muslin-lined sieve into a bowl, leave to cool briefly, then discard any mussels that haven't opened. Shell the rest and set aside. Return the stock to the pan and simmer over a moderate heat, then stir in the cream and season to taste. Add the monkfish, cook for 2–3 minutes, then the sole for 1 minute, then the vegetables and mussels for a final 2 minutes.

**4** Using a slotted spoon, distribute the vegetables between the bowls. Place the fish on top, ladle over the broth and scatter with mussels. Sprinkle with chopped tarragon and the reserved spring onion. Serve hot.

**SERVES** 4      **PREP** 20 MINS **COOK** 30 MINS

This rustic, Mediterranean-style fish soup – robustly flavoured with brandy, orange, and fennel – is simple to prepare and sure to please.

# Fish soup with fennel

30g (1oz) butter

3 tbsp olive oil

1 large fennel bulb, finely chopped

2 garlic cloves, crushed

1 small leek, sliced

4 ripe plum tomatoes, chopped

3 tbsp brandy

¼ tsp saffron threads, infused in a little hot water

zest of ½ orange

1 bay leaf

1.7 litres (3 pints) fish stock

300g (10oz) potatoes, diced and parboiled for 5 minutes

4 tbsp dry white wine

500g (1lb 2oz) fresh black mussels, scrubbed and debearded

salt and freshly ground black pepper

500g (1lb 2oz) monkfish or firm white fish, cut into bite-sized pieces

6 raw whole tiger prawns

parsley, chopped, to garnish

**1** Heat the butter with 2 tbsp of the oil in a large, deep pan. Stir in the fennel, garlic, and leek, and fry over a moderate heat, stirring occasionally, for 5 minutes, or until softened and lightly browned.

**2** Stir in the tomatoes, add the brandy, and boil rapidly for 2 minutes, or until the juices are reduced slightly. Stir in the saffron, orange zest, bay leaf, fish stock, and potatoes. Bring to the boil, then reduce the heat and skim off any scum from the surface. Cover and simmer for 20 minutes, or until the potatoes are tender. Remove the bay leaf.

**3** Meanwhile, heat the remaining oil with the wine in a large, deep pan until boiling. Add the mussels, cover, and continue on high heat for 2–3 minutes, shaking the pan often. Discard any mussels that do not open. Strain, reserving the liquid, and set the mussels aside. Add the liquid to the soup and season to taste. Bring to the boil, add the monkfish and prawns, then reduce the heat, cover, and simmer gently for 5 minutes, or until the fish is just cooked and the prawns are pink. Add the mussels to the pan and bring almost to the boil. Serve the soup sprinkled with chopped parsley.

**SERVES** 4–6    **PREP** 10 MINS **COOK** 1 HOUR

The subtle combinations of meaty monkfish, delicate haddock, aniseed fennel, and the light scent of saffron marry well. You could add some mussels or prawns, if you like.

# Rich fish soup

1 tbsp olive oil
1 onion, finely chopped
salt and freshly ground black pepper
1 sprig of thyme
3 garlic cloves, finely chopped
1 fennel bulb, trimmed and finely chopped
1 red chilli, deseeded and finely chopped
250ml (9fl oz) dry white wine

2 x 400g cans chopped tomatoes
900ml (1½ pints) hot light vegetable stock
pinch of saffron threads
200g (7oz) monkfish, cut into
   bite-sized pieces
200g (7oz) haddock loin, cut into
   bite-sized pieces

**1** Heat the oil in a large heavy-based pan over a medium heat, add the onion, and cook for 3–4 minutes until soft. Season with salt and pepper and throw in the thyme. Add the garlic and fennel, and cook gently for a further 5 minutes until the fennel begins to soften.

**2** Stir through the chilli and cook for 1 minute, then increase the heat, add the wine, let it bubble for a minute, and then tip in the canned tomatoes and stock. Add the saffron, bring to the boil, then reduce to a simmer and cook gently, partially covered with the lid, for about 45 minutes. Take care that the sauce doesn't dry out, topping it up with a little hot water if needed.

**3** Use a stick blender to blend the soup until smooth, or transfer in batches to a liquidizer and blend until smooth, and return to a clean pan. Top up with a little hot water – you will probably need about 300ml (10fl oz) in total – and simmer gently. Taste and season as needed, add the fish, put the lid back on, and cook on a low heat for 6–10 minutes or until the fish is opaque and cooked through. Ladle into warmed bowls and serve with white crusty bread. Garnish with chopped fennel fronds, if you like.

**SERVES** 4–6      **PREP** 15 MINS **COOK** 1 HOUR      **FREEZE** UP TO 1 MONTH

A rich broth sets off the sweetness of the scallops while the chorizo (or black pudding) adds a spicy contrast. Serve as the first course of a dinner party menu.

# Creamy scallop bisque

300ml (10fl oz) dry white wine
15g (½oz) butter
1 small onion, finely chopped
1 small shallot, very finely chopped
1 medium-sized ripe tomato, chopped
200g (7oz) prawns, shelled
100g (3½oz) cod or pollock, skinned
  and cut into chunks
12 small scallops (or 6 large), white
  parts and corals

2 tbsp chopped parsley
2 tsp dill seeds
sea salt and freshly ground black pepper
3 tbsp brandy
100ml (3½fl oz) single cream
75g (2½oz) chorizo, diced, or black
  pudding, minced
1 tbsp finely chopped chives, to finish

**1** Boil 700ml (1¼ pints) water with the wine. Put the butter in a sauté pan over a medium heat. Add the onion and shallot and soften until golden. Add the tomato, prawns, fish, corals, parsley, and dill seeds. Stir, and cook for 5 minutes. Stir in the brandy, and cook for a minute. Pour in the boiling wine mixture and season lightly. Reduce the heat, and simmer gently for 10 minutes. Take off the heat and leave to cool. Stir and mash down the soup with the back of a spoon. Then gently heat the cream in another pan until hot.

**2** Transfer the soup to a blender and purée. Strain through a sieve back into the pan and stir in the hot cream. Return to a simmer. Remove from the heat and adjust the seasoning. Cover and keep warm.

**3** Put a non-stick frying pan over a medium heat. Add the chorizo or black pudding and fry for 3–5 minutes until cooked through and crispy. Set aside on a plate lined with kitchen paper and keep warm.

**4** Add the scallops to the pan. Cook for 2 minutes, turn over and cook for a minute. Remove from the heat. Ladle the soup into 4 bowls and add the scallops. Scatter over the chorizo or black pudding and serve immediately.

**SERVES** 4    **PREP** 20 MINS **COOK** 40 MINS

Buy your crab ready cooked or, for optimum freshness, buy it live and cook it yourself. Boiling is the most common way to cook a live crab, although they can also be steamed.

# Crab bisque

1 cooked spider crab or velvet crab, about 1kg (2¼lb) in weight
50g (1¾oz) butter
olive oil
1 onion, finely chopped
1 carrot, finely chopped
2 celery stalks, finely chopped
1 leek, finely chopped
½ fennel bulb, finely chopped
1 bay leaf
1 sprig of tarragon
2 garlic cloves, crushed

2.5cm (1in) fresh ginger, peeled and finely chopped
75g (2½ oz) tomato purée
4 tomatoes, roughly chopped
120ml (4fl oz) Cognac or brandy
100ml (3½ fl oz) dry white wine or vermouth
1.7 litres (3 pints) fish stock
120ml (4fl oz) cream
salt and freshly ground black pepper
pinch of cayenne pepper
juice of ½ lemon
chopped chives, to garnish

**1** Remove the crab meat from the shell and chop into small pieces. Chop the shell up roughly and put shell and meat to one side. Heat the butter and oil in a large saucepan over a medium heat. Add the vegetables, herbs, garlic, and ginger. Cook, stirring occasionally, for 10 minutes or until softened.

**2** Add the chopped shell, then stir in the tomato purée, tomatoes, Cognac, wine, and stock. Bring to the boil and simmer for 1 hour. Leave to cool slightly, then blend till smooth. Strain through a coarse sieve, pushing as much liquid through as you can with the back of a ladle, and then put through a fine sieve.

**3** Return the soup to the pan and bring to the boil. Add the crab meat and cream, then season to taste with salt and pepper, and add cayenne and lemon juice to taste. Garnish with chives and serve in warm bowls.

**SERVES** 4    **PREP** 45 MINS **COOK** 1 HOUR 10 MINS    **FREEZE** UP TO 2 MONTHS
BEFORE CREAM IS ADDED

The name 'bisque' refers to a rich and luxurious shellfish soup with cream and brandy and is thought to have come from the Spanish Biscay region.

# Lobster bisque

1 lobster, cooked, about 1kg (2¼lb) in weight
50g (1¾oz) butter
1 onion, finely chopped
1 carrot, finely chopped
2 celery sticks, finely chopped
1 leek, finely chopped
½ fennel bulb, finely chopped
1 bay leaf
1 sprig of tarragon
2 garlic cloves, crushed

75g (2½oz) tomato purée
4 tomatoes, roughly chopped
120ml (4fl oz) Cognac or brandy
100ml (3½fl oz) dry white wine or vermouth
1.7 litres (3 pints) fish stock
120ml (4fl oz) cream
salt and freshly ground black pepper
pinch of cayenne
juice of ½ lemon
chives, to garnish

**1** Split the lobster in half, remove the meat from the body and chop the meat into small pieces. Twist off the claws and legs, break at the joints and remove the meat, then crack all the shells with the back of a knife. Chop the shells into rough pieces and put the meat into the refrigerator.

**2** Melt the butter in a large pan over a medium heat, add the vegetables, herbs and garlic, and cook for 10 minutes, or until softened, stirring occasionally. Add the lobster shells. Stir in the tomato purée, tomatoes, Cognac, white wine and fish stock. Bring to the boil and simmer for 1 hour.

**3** Leave to cool slightly, then ladle into a food processor. Process in short bursts, until the shell breaks into very small pieces. Strain through a coarse sieve, pushing through as much as you can, then pass it again through a fine sieve before returning to the heat.

**4** Bring to the boil, add the reserved lobster meat and the cream, then season to taste, adding the cayenne and lemon. Serve in warm bowls, garnished with chives.

**SERVES** 4     **PREP** 45 MINS **COOK** 1 HOUR 10 MINS     **FREEZE** UP TO 2 MONTHS
BEFORE THE CREAM IS ADDED

This fragrant soup takes the best ingredients from a cottage garden in the southern Indian state of Kerala. If you are using dried curry leaves, add them with the stock.

# Keralan prawn soup

1 tsp black peppercorns
¾ tsp mustard seeds
2 tsp coriander seeds
½ tsp fenugreek seeds
2–3 large red chillies
4 garlic cloves, chopped
5cm (2in) fresh root ginger, chopped
4 tbsp hot water
2–3 tbsp vegetable oil

small handful of fresh curry leaves
2 onions, finely chopped
750ml (1¼ pints) fish stock
250ml (8fl oz) coconut milk
250g (9oz) raw king prawns, shelled
1 tbsp coconut cream
2 tbsp fresh coriander leaves, chopped
juice of 1 lime, to taste

**1** Heat a sturdy frying pan or small griddle over a low heat. Roast the peppercorns, mustard, coriander and fenugreek seeds for about 30 seconds, until they give off a spicy aroma and the mustard seeds start to pop. Grind the spices to a powder using a mortar and pestle, and set aside.

**2** Roughly chop the chillies – if you like a mild flavour, use just 2 chillies and remove the seeds. Put the chillies in a small food processor with the garlic and ginger. Pour in the hot water and process to a paste. Set aside.

**3** Heat the oil in a wok or saucepan. When hot, toss in the curry leaves and fry for 20 seconds, Be careful – curry leaves spit when added to hot oil. Add the onions, cover and soften for 10 minutes, stirring occasionally.

**4** Stir in the chilli, garlic and ginger paste and fry for 2–3 minutes, until the water evaporates. Add the ground spice mixture and cook for a further 30 seconds, stirring all the time. Pour in the stock and simmer for 20 minutes or until reduced by one-third. Stir in the coconut milk and reheat before adding the prawns and cooking for a further 4–5 minutes. Add the coconut cream and finish with the coriander leaves and enough lime juice to sharpen.

**SERVES** 4–6  **PREP** 20 MINS **COOK** 40 MINS

This version is quicker than the traditional method of slow-simmering a whole chicken. Some cock-a-leekie recipes use prunes – try adding a few with the vegetables in step 2.

# Cock-a-leekie soup

450g (1lb) chicken breasts
    and thighs, skinned
2 bay leaves
1 litre (1¾ pints) chicken or
    vegetable stock
60g (2oz) long-grain rice
2 leeks, thinly sliced
2 carrots, grated
pinch of ground cloves
1 tsp sea salt
1 tbsp chopped fresh parsley

**1** PLace the chicken in a large pan with the bay leaves and pour over the stock. Bring to the boil, then reduce the heat, cover the pan, and simmer for 30 minutes.

**2** Skim the surface of the soup and discard any scum that has formed. Add the rice, leeks, carrots, cloves, and salt. Bring back to the boil, reduce the heat, cover the pan, and simmer for a further 30 minutes.

**3** Remove the bay leaves and discard. If you wish, lift out the chicken, remove the meat from the bones, then return the meat to the soup. Ladle the soup into a warm tureen or divide between individual serving bowls, and serve hot, garnished with parsley.

**SERVES** 4    **PREP** 10 MINS **COOK** 1¼ HOURS    **FREEZE** UP TO 3 MONTHS

This is a traditional soup with a modern twist. Adding baking powder and mashed potato to the balls gives them a really light, fluffy texture.

# Matzo ball soup

1 chicken leg and thigh portion
1 onion, finely chopped
1 leek, thinly sliced
1 large carrot, finely diced
1 litre (1¾ pints) water
1 sprig of fresh thyme
1 tsp celery salt
salt and freshly ground black pepper

½ tsp grated fresh root ginger
1 tbsp chopped fresh thyme
1 tbsp chopped fresh parsley
1 garlic clove, finely chopped
salt and freshly ground black pepper
1 tbsp sunflower oil
1 egg, beaten
4 small sprigs of fresh thyme, to garnish

**For the matzo balls**
1 potato, about 115g (4oz),
   cooked and mashed
45g (1½oz) fine matzo meal
½ tsp baking powder

**1** Put the soup ingredients in a large saucepan. Bring to the boil, reduce the heat, cover, and simmer gently for 1 hour, topping up with water if it gets low. Meanwhile, mix the mashed potato with the matzo meal, baking powder, ginger, thyme, parsley, garlic, and a little salt and pepper. Add the oil then mix with the beaten egg to form a soft, slightly sticky dough. Shape into 8 balls.

**2** Discard the thyme sprig from the soup. Carefully lift out the chicken and remove all meat from the bones, discarding the skin. Chop the flesh and return to the soup. Taste and adjust the seasoning, if necessary.

**3** Bring the soup back to a simmer, drop in the balls, cover, and simmer gently for about 10 minutes until fluffy and cooked through. Ladle into warm soup bowls and garnish each with a small sprig of fresh thyme.

**SERVES** 4     **PREP** 15 MINS **COOK** 1 HOUR 10 MINS     **FREEZE** UP TO 3 MONTHS
                                                                                   BROTH ONLY

Make thrifty use of leftover turkey by simmering your own stock with the carcase after a roast dinner. This broth is every bit as appealing when made with chicken.

# Turkey broth

1 litre (1¾ pints) turkey stock or
    chicken stock
120ml (4fl oz) dry white wine
1 carrot, finely diced
1 parsnip, finely diced
2 celery stalks, finely diced
1 leek (white part only), finely diced
1 small turnip, finely diced
salt and freshly ground black pepper
225g (8oz) cooked turkey meat, finely diced
100ml (3½fl oz) single cream
2 tbsp chopped parsley
crusty bread, to serve

**1** Bring the stock and wine to the boil in a large pan, then stir in the carrot, parsnip, celery, leek, and turnip. Season with salt and freshly ground black pepper, half-cover with a lid, and simmer for 20 minutes.

**2** Stir in the cooked turkey, cream, and chopped parsley and reheat gently. Serve the soup with plenty of crusty bread.

**SERVES** 6    **PREP** 20 MINS **COOK** 25 MINS    ❄ **FREEZE** UP TO 3 MONTHS
BEFORE CREAM IS ADDED

The warming flavours of steak and onions make this soup a rich and satisfying meal. For an authentic touch, use Hungarian paprika – it is fairly readily available these days.

# Hungarian goulash soup

120ml (4fl oz) olive oil
675g (1½lb) onions, thinly sliced
2 garlic cloves, crushed
675g (1½lb) chuck steak, cut into
   5cm (2in) cubes
salt and freshly ground black pepper
2 tbsp paprika
1 tsp caraway seeds
1 tsp cayenne pepper, plus extra to garnish
4 tbsp tomato purée
1 litre (1¾ pints) beef stock
soured cream, to garnish

**1** Heat 3 tbsp of the olive oil in a large casserole over a medium heat, add the onions, and cook, stirring occasionally, for 10 minutes or until they are golden brown. Add the garlic for the final 2 minutes, then remove the casserole from the heat.

**2** Heat the remaining oil in a frying pan, add the steak, and cook, stirring often, for 5 minutes or until brown on all sides. Season with salt and add to the onions, along with the spices and tomato purée. Return the casserole to the heat and cook for 5 minutes, stirring all the time, then pour in the stock. Cover with a lid and simmer gently for 1¾ hours.

**3** Season to taste with salt and freshly ground black pepper, then serve the soup garnished with soured cream, a sprinkling of cayenne, and some more freshly ground black pepper.

**SERVES** 6–8     **PREP** 15 MINS **COOK** 2 HOURS     **FREEZE** UP TO 3 MONTHS
                                                        AT THE END OF STEP 2

A favourite from Goa in southern India, the vindaloo is Portuguese in heritage and notable for its garlicky masala, spiked with wine vinegar and softened with sugar.

# Pork vindaloo broth

6 dried red chillies
650g (1½lb) boneless pork belly with rind, cut into 2.5 x 5cm (1 x 2in) chunks
1 tsp cumin seeds
½ tsp black peppercorns
6 garlic cloves, roughly chopped
5cm (2 in) fresh root ginger, roughly chopped
1 tsp sweet paprika
3 tbsp tamarind pulp
3 tbsp white wine vinegar
4–6 tbsp vegetable oil

5cm (2in) cinnamon stick
2 star anise
3 onions, finely chopped
175ml (6 fl oz) white wine
1.7 litres (3 pints) chicken stock
2–3 tsp date palm sugar or dark muscovado sugar, to taste
salt
1 red chilli, deseeded and cut into strips, to serve
2 tbsp fresh coriander leaves, to serve

**1** Soak the chillies in hot water for 10 minutes (for a mild flavour, remove the seeds first). Put the pork in a pan, cover with boiling water, bring to the boil and simmer for 5 minutes. Drain, discard the liquid, and set aside.

**2** Dry-roast the cumin and peppercorns (see page127) and grind using a mortar and pestle. In a small food processor, process the ground spices, drained red chillies, garlic, ginger, paprika, tamarind, and vinegar. Set aside.

**3** Heat the oil in a pan. When hot, fry the cinnamon and star anise for 30 seconds. Add the onions and fry for 10–15 minutes. Add the spice paste and cook for 1 minute. Pour in the wine and stock and bring to the boil. Add the pork, turn the heat down low, and simmer for 2 hours. Chill overnight.

**4** Next day, scoop out the meat, strip away the rind, and dice. Skim the fat from the stock and strain the liquid into a clean pan. Bring to a fast boil over a high heat and cook for 5–10 minutes. Sweeten with sugar and season with salt. Before serving, stir in the pork and garnish with the chilli strips and coriander leaves.

**SERVES** 6     **PREP** 35 MINS PLUS OVERNIGHT CHILLING     **FREEZE** UP TO 3 MONTHS
**COOK** 3 HOURS     WITHOUT THE GARNISH

An Anglo-Indian soup from colonial days, mulligatawny has many variations. For extra heat, pop a split red chilli in the pan when you pour over the stock.

# Mulligatawny

40g (1¼oz) butter
1 large onion, chopped
5cm (2in) fresh root ginger, finely chopped
2 garlic cloves, finely chopped
1 cox apple, unpeeled, diced, with peel
1 carrot, sliced
1 celery stick, sliced
1 heaped tbsp mild curry powder
1 tbsp gram flour or plain flour

4 tomatoes, roughly chopped
2 tsp tomato purée
500ml (16fl oz) hot chicken stock
2 bay leaves
salt and freshly ground black pepper
200ml (7fl oz) coconut milk or single cream
175g (7oz) cooked chicken meat, shredded
juice of ½ lime
2 tbsp chopped fresh coriander

**1** Melt the butter in a large pan and soften the onion, ginger, and garlic for 10 minutes, without colouring. Add the apple, carrot, and celery to the pan and continue cooking, covered, for 5 minutes.

**2** Stir in the curry powder and fry for 1 minute, stirring all the time. Sprinkle over the gram flour (or plain flour) and continue cooking for another 20 seconds.

**3** Add the tomatoes and tomato purée followed by the chicken stock. Add the bay leaves and season with salt and pepper. Bring to the boil, stirring, then reduce the heat and simmer, half-covered for 20 minutes.

**4** Remove the bay leaf and blend until smooth, using a stick blender or liquidizer. Sieve the soup to remove any fibres and skin. Reheat, stir in the coconut milk or cream, and add the diced chicken. Sharpen with a squeeze of lime and add the chopped coriander.

**SERVES** 4 **PREP** 20 MINS **COOK** 45 MINS **FREEZE** UP TO 3 MONTHS

Enriched with sherry, this slow-cooked soup is a classic for flavourful comfort eating. If you prefer a chunky texture, the soup also tastes good unblended.

# Oxtail soup

2 tbsp vegetable oil
salt and freshly ground black pepper
600g (1lb 5oz) ox tails, disjointed,
   available from your butcher
1 onion, sliced
2 carrots, diced
2 celery sticks, diced

400g (14oz) tin chopped tomatoes
¼ bunch of parsley
1 bay leaf
2 sprigs of fresh thyme
1 tbsp plain flour
1 tbsp butter
150ml (5fl oz) dry sherry

**1** Heat the oil in a large saucepan, season the ox tails with salt and pepper, add them to the hot oil, and fry until golden on all sides. Add the onion and fry until softened slightly. Add 2 litres of water, season with salt and pepper, and simmer, uncovered, for about 2 hours. Cover and continue to simmer for a further 2 hours. Check to see if the liquid needs topping up during cooking.

**2** Add the carrots, celery, and tomatoes. Tie the parsley, bay leaf, and thyme sprigs together with kitchen string, and place in the pan. Bring to the boil and simmer for 30 minutes, or until the vegetables are tender.

**3** Remove the herb bundle and discard. Scoop out the meat, remove from the bones, and discard the skin and bones. Strain the stock, reserving the vegetables. Refrigerate the stock for an hour or more. Using a blender, whiz the meat and vegetables and set aside.

**4** Once the stock is chilled, remove the fat from the top and discard. Reheat the stock. In a large, dry frying pan, brown the flour over a high heat. Cool slightly. Add the butter and blend. A little at a time, stir in the stock and the meat–vegetable purée. Season with salt and pepper to taste, and add the sherry just before serving.

This flavoursome Portuguese soup is thickened with potatoes and makes a perfect supper dish for the colder months. It is also fairly healthy, and filled with greens. The quantity of linguiça sausage may seem small, but gives the perfect amount of piquancy and substance to the soup.

# Caldo verde

5 tbsp olive oil
1 onion, finely chopped
3 garlic cloves, crushed
150g (5½oz) linguiça (about 3), skinned and finely diced
800g (1¾lb) potatoes, peeled, halved, and finely sliced

1.2 litres (2 pints) good-quality chicken stock
salt and freshly ground black pepper
200g (7oz) dark green cabbage leaves, cavolo nero, or curly kale, washed and shredded
¼ tsp smoked paprika

**1** In a large, heavy saucepan, heat 4 tablespoons of the oil. Add the onion and fry over a medium heat for 5 minutes, until softened. Add the garlic and linguiça and cook for 2–3 minutes, until the sausage releases its oil. Stir in the potatoes.

**2** Add the stock and bring to the boil. Season with pepper and a little salt if necessary, reduce the heat, cover, and simmer for 20 minutes. The potatoes should be breaking up.

**3** Blanch the cabbage in boiling salted water for 1–2 minutes, until softened. Drain and rinse in cold water. Mash the potatoes into the soup until it is smooth and thick. Add the cabbage and cook for 5 minutes.

**4** Heat the remaining oil in a small saucepan. Take from the heat and stir in the paprika. Serve the soup in warmed bowls with a swirl of the spicy paprika oil on top, and plenty of crusty bread.

**SERVES** 4 **PREP** 10 MINS **COOK** 35 MINS

Alfonso mangoes, renowned for their fragrant flesh and creamy texture, have a short season from early April until the end of May. Other varieties work well too.

# Mango and curry leaf soup

**For the garnish**
small handful of curry leaves
vegetable oil for deep frying

**For the soup**
4 ripe mangoes, Alfonso if in season, available from South Asian stores
2 tbsp vegetable oil
1 tsp black mustard seeds
handful of fresh curry leaves

1 red chilli, deseeded, finely chopped
2 tsp date palm sugar or dark muscovado sugar
½ tsp turmeric
2 tsp rice flour
300–400ml (10–14fl oz) vegetable stock
300ml (10fl oz) coconut milk
juice of 1 lime, to taste
salt and freshly ground black pepper
2 tbsp chopped fresh coriander leaves

**1** First make the garnish: deep-fry the curry leaves in hot oil until crisp – it only takes a few seconds. Drain on kitchen paper and set aside.

**2** Roughly chop the flesh of 3 mangoes into small pieces and finely dice the fourth. Set aside. Heat the oil in a medium pan and, when hot, fry the mustard seeds for a few seconds before adding the curry leaves and chilli. Continue frying for 30 seconds, until the leaves stop spluttering.

**3** Add the 3 roughly chopped mangoes to the pan, reserving the diced mango. Turn the heat down low and simmer the fruit until softened. Stir in the sugar and cook until the mango begins to caramelize. Sprinkle over the turmeric and rice flour and fry for 30 seconds, stirring all the time. Pour over 300ml (10fl oz) of the stock and simmer for 10 minutes.

**4** Add the coconut milk and simmer for 2–3 minutes. Sharpen with lime juice, season with salt and pepper, and stir in the coriander leaves and diced mango. If the soup is too thick, add a little hot vegetable stock. Divide the soup between the bowls and sprinkle with a few crisp-fried curry leaves.

**SERVES** 4     **PREP** 15 MINS **COOK** 20 MINS     **FREEZE** UP TO 1 MONTH
AT THE END OF STEP 3

Various basic cooking methods are used in preparing stews and casseroles. Poaching involves gentle simmering in water, braising is excellent for sealing in flavour, stewing produces wonderful sauces where the ingredients have melded together, and pot roasting is ideal for cooking whole joints of meat.

# Basic cooking methods

## poaching

The ingredients are immersed in water, then simmered very gently. This works well for both delicate meats, such as fish or chicken breast, and dense or tougher meats, such as silverside of beef; a clean, silky texture is achieved. A fitted lid is essential for keeping the moisture in the pan. Never attempt to rush poaching – hard boiling dries out meat..

**1** Use enough cold water to cover the meat, then bring the water to the boil. Add a pinch of salt and the meat. reduce the heat and bring back to a gentle simmer, cover the pan with the lid, and poach for 30 minutes.

**2** Add vegetables to flavour the stock, such as artichokes, carrots, broad beans, and any other green vegetables you want to include – maybe shredded cabbage or runner beans – and cook for 5–10 minutes until they are tender.

**3** To test the chicken for doneness, pierce the thigh to the bone – if the juices run clear it is done, if they are red it is not. Tip the bird slightly as you lift it out of the pan so that the hot stock in its cavity runs back into the pan.

# braising

This technique combines both dry heat and moist heat cooking. The meat, poultry, or vegetables are first seared in hot fat and then cooked slowly in a pan with minimal liquid – just enough to cover. Searing helps the meat to remain succulent. The meat is cut into slightly larger pieces than it would be for stewing. Slightly more expensive cuts can be used for braising, although this technique works just as well with cheap cuts. Braising suits cuts such as brisket, shanks, and oxtail very well.

1 Heat the oil in a frying pan over a medium-high heat and brown the meat. Let the pieces sit for about 5 minutes until brown underneath, then turn them and cook the other side for another 5 minutes. Remove with a slotted spoon and set aside.

2 Add a mixture of aromatic vegetables, such as carrots, onions, celery, and leeks, stir well with a spatula to collect the meat residue, then cook until the vegetables are browned. Add flavourings, such as thyme, bay leaves, and garlic, and continue to cook for a few minutes more.

3 Put the meat and vegetables in a flameproof casserole, pour in some wine, and boil over a high heat until nearly evaporated. Add enough stock to cover the meat. Bring to a simmer, cover with the lid, and cook in the oven on a low heat until the meat is tender.

Most vegetables are suited to stews and casseroles, although some need longer cooking than others. Knowing how to prepare vegetables correctly saves time and is key to a successful dish.

# Preparing vegetables

### peeling and chopping garlic

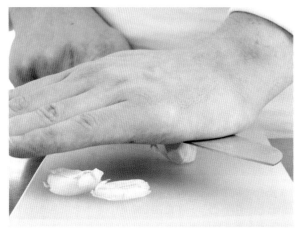

**1** Place each garlic clove flat on a cutting board Place the flat of a large knife blade on top and pound it with the heel of your hand.

**2** Discard the skin and cut off the ends of each clove. Slice the clove into slivers lengthways, then cut across into tiny chunks. Collect the pieces into a pile and chop again for finer pieces.

### peeling and dicing onions

**1** Cut onion in half and peel it, leaving the root to hold the layers together. Make a few slices into the onion, but not through the root.

**2** With the tip of your knife, slice down through the layers of onion vertically, cutting as close to the root as possible.

**3** Cut across the vertical slices to produce even dice. Use the root to hold the onion steady, then cut off when all the onion is diced.

# skinning and deseeding tomatoes

f **1** Remove the green stem, score an "X" in the skin
ι of each tomato at the base, then immerse it in a
s pan of boiling water for 20 seconds, or until the
skin loosens.

**2** Using a slotted spoon, remove the tomato from
the pan of boiling water and place it into a bowl of
iced water to cool.

**13** When cool enough to handle, use a paring knife
l to peel away the loosened skin.

**4** Cut each tomato in half and gently squeeze out
the seeds over a bowl. Discard the seeds.

## peeling squashes

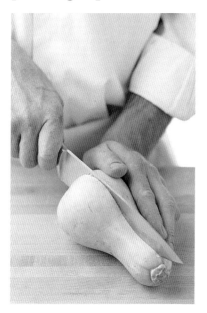  

**1** Holding the squash firmly, use a chef's knife to cut it lengthways in half, working from the stalk to the core.

**2** Using a spoon, remove the seeds and fibres from each squash half and discard them.

**3** Use a vegetable peeler or knife to remove the skin. Cut into pieces, then into chunks, or slice as required.

## rehydrating mushrooms

**1** Place the mushrooms – either wild or cultivated – into a bowl of hot water. Allow them to soak for at least 15 minutes.

**2** Use a slotted spoon to remove mushrooms from soaking liquid. If using the soaking liquid in your recipe, strain it to remove any sand or grit.

Herbs and spices are essential for adding aroma and flavour to stews and casseroles. Experience will teach you which spices to use with which foods, so use them sparingly at first. Add woody herbs, such as thyme and bay, at the beginning of cooking; but delicate ones, such as parsley and mint, are best added at the end as they can lose their potency. Chillies, on the other hand, can intensify with cooking.

# Using herbs and spices

### making a bouquet garni

This is a bundle of herbs used to flavour a sauce. For a classic combination, tie sprigs of thyme and parsley and a bay leaf together. You could also include sage or rosemary.

### deseeding and cutting chillies

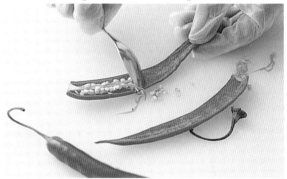

Slice chillies in half lengthways then scrape out the seeds (this will reduce their heat, so leave if you wish). Slice or chop finely; wearing plastic gloves is a good idea.

### dry-roasting spices

To dry-roast spices, such as cloves, star anise and cinnamon, place in an oven at 160°C (325°F/Gas 3), or fry in a dry pan until lightly browned.

### frying spices in oil

Frying spices until lightly coloured, traps their flavour in the oil. This is called tempering. The oil is used with the spices at the start or end of cooking.

The hard exteriors of dried pulses need long simmering to soften, making them a natural choice for stews and casseroles. The basic preparation of pulses is simple – sort, rinse, soak if needed, and simmer. They can then be used for different dishes, including favourites from around the world such as chilli (see pp146–7), the fragrant dahls of the India (see p155) and Spain's grand meat and vegetable stew Cocido (see pp216–17).

# Preparing pulses

### sorting and rinsing

Whatever kind of pulse you're using, whether beans, lentils, whole peas, or split peas, start by sorting and rinsing them. Place the pulses in a colander and carefully pick out any damaged or broken ones, and any foreign material such as husks, pieces of grit, or tiny pebbles. Then rinse the pulses well under cold running water. Rinsing is essential for removing excess dust and dirt from the pulses.

### soaking

Apart from lentils and split peas, all pulses need to be soaked for at least 8 hours, and preferably overnight (you will find that old pulses need soaking for longer, so it is best to plan to leave them overnight). Soaking enables pulses to cook more quickly and evenly. Place them in a bowl, add three times their volume of cold water, then cover and place in the refrigerator. When you are ready to cook, drain the pulses and discard the soaking water.

# boiling

Drain the soaked pulses, then place them in a large pan along with any flavourings. Pour in four times their volume of cold water and add 1 tbsp of vegetable oil to stop them sticking. Bring rapidly to the boil, and boil hard for 10 minutes, skimming away any foam with a slotted spoon. (Some pulses, such as kidney beans, contain toxins that are destroyed by this initial 10 minutes of hard boiling.) Lower the heat, part-cover with a lid, and simmer until tender, or transfer to the slow cooker to cook.

# adding flavour

The flavour of pulses can be rather bland, so it's usually a good idea to add some aromatics. A bouquet garni or a sprig of herbs will do the trick: bay leaf, parsley, rosemary, or thyme all work well. A pinch of cumin, coriander, chilli, or caraway is another option, but you can also pop a carrot into the pan, or an onion studded with cloves. Alternatively, you can cook pulses in a well flavoured stock, but never season it with salt – it will prevent them from softening.

## SOAKING AND COOKING TIMES

Use the following soaking and cooking times to prepare pulses. Remember, however, that the cooking times given are only a general guide, and may vary slightly, depending on how old the pulses you are using are.

| Type of pulse | Soaking time | Approximate cooking time |
| --- | --- | --- |
| Adzuki beans | overnight | 40–45 mins |
| Black beans | overnight | 1 hr |
| Black-eyed peas | overnight | 1–1½ hrs |
| Borlotti beans | overnight | 1–1½ hrs |
| Butter beans | overnight | 1–1½ hrs |
| Cannellini beans | overnight | 1–1½ hrs |
| Chickpeas | overnight | 2–3 hrs |
| Flageolet beans | overnight | 1½ hrs |
| Haricot beans | overnight | 1–1½ hrs |
| Lentils (split) | not required | 25 mins |
| Lentils (whole) | not required | 45 mins |
| Pinto beans | overnight | 1–1½ hrs |
| Kidney beans | boil hard for 10 mins, then soak for 4 hrs | 1–1½ hrs |
| Split peas | not required | 45 mins |

The following techniques show you how to truss a bird for pot roasting, how to debone it, and how to joint it into portions that are perfect for stews and casseroles.

# Preparing poultry

## trussing

This can appear fiddly but once mastered, it only takes minutes to do. Trussing a bird before cooking allows it to hold its shape and helps to cook it evenly, without overcooking any of the bony parts first.

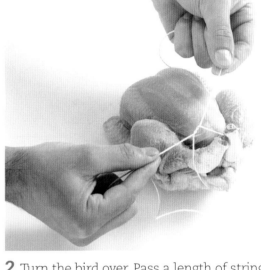

**1** Season the insides of the bird with salt and pepper. Holding the bird breast-side down on a clean work surface, tuck the neck skin under the bird, and fold the wings over it.

**2** Turn the bird over. Pass a length of string und the tail end; tie a secure knot over the leg joint Bring the strings along the sides, between the breast and legs, and loop them round the legs.

**3** Turn the bird over again and tie the strings under the body. Bring both ends of string down between the sides of the body and the wings.

**4** Tie the wing bones at the neck opening so they are tucked securely under the body. After cooking, cut the string to remove it.

# deboning poultry

If you prefer boneless meat, leg pieces (shown here) are better for stews and casseroles than the leaner breast meat. You may also wish to remove the bone to stuff the meat. Use a good, sharp knife and a series of shallow cuts to free the bone while preserving all the flesh.

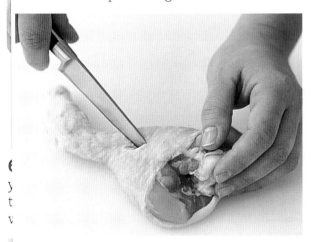

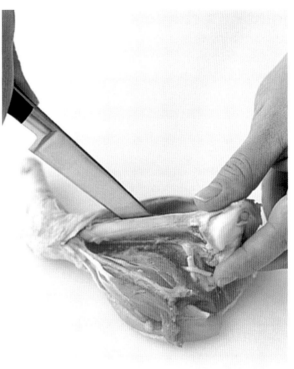

**1** To debone a drumstick, start in the middle and insert the tip of your knife until you locate the bone. Slice along the bone in both directions to expose it fully.

**2** Open the flesh and cut neatly around the bone using short strokes to free it completely from the flesh. Discard the bone, or use it to flavour stock.

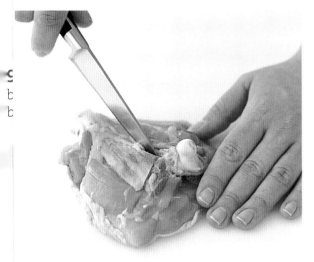

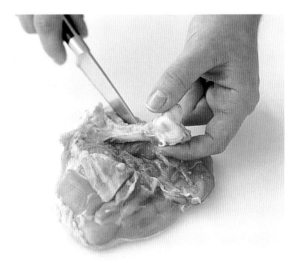

**3** To debone a thigh, place it skin-side down on a cutting board. Using a small, sharp knife, cut away the flesh to expose the thigh bone.

**4** Cut an incision through the flesh, following the contour of the exposed bone. Cut around the bone to free it from the flesh.

An essential tool for preparing fish is a filleting knife, which has a long, flexible blade. This makes it easy to remove the skin and cut through bones. Always buy good quality fresh fish and buy seafood on the day you intend to cook it. Clean seafood thoroughly.

# Preparing fish and seafood

### scaling and trimming fish

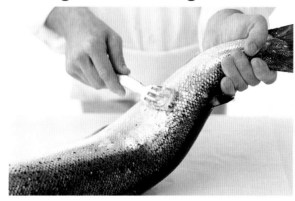

**1** Lay the fish on top of a clean work surface Holding the fish by the tail, scrape the scales off with a fish scaler or the blade of a chef's knife, using strokes towards the head.

**2** Once the fish is descaled, use kitchen scissors to remove the dorsal (back) fin, the belly fins, and the two fins on either side of the head.

### filleting and skinning a fish

**1** Gut the fish through the stomach. Cut into the head at an angle, just behind the gills, down to the backbone. Move to top of the fish and cut down the length of each side of the backbone.

**2** Place fillet skin-side down on a work surface. Insert a filleting knife into the flesh at the tail end. Hold the skin taut and, with the blade held almost parallel to the skin, cut off the flesh.

# preparing mussels

**1** Discard any mussels that are broken or wide open. In the sink, scrub the mussels under cold, running water. Rinse away grit or sand and remove any barnacles with a small, sharp knife.

**2** To remove the dark stringy "beard", pinch it between your fingers, pull it away from the mussel, and discard. If a mussel is not tightly closed, tap it to check it is fresh; if it doesn't close when tapped, discard.

# peeling and deveining prawns

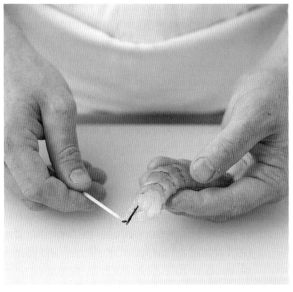

**1** Remove the head and legs by pulling them off with your fingers, then peel away the shells. Save the shells for stock, if you like.

**2** Using the tip of a paring knife or cocktail stick, hook the vein where the head was and gently pull it away from the body.

Dumplings are the perfect addition to a casserole or stew as they make the dish a complete meal. For variety, add other herbs, such as thyme or tarragon, to the parsley in the mixture.

# Vegetable casserole with dumplings

1 tbsp olive oil
1 onion, roughly chopped
salt and freshly ground black pepper
3 garlic cloves, finely chopped
pinch of dried chilli flakes
2 leeks, trimmed and thickly sliced
3 carrots, peeled and roughly chopped
2 celery sticks, roughly chopped

1 tbsp plain flour
900ml (1½ pints) hot vegetable stock
400g can haricot beans, drained and rinsed
few sprigs of rosemary
225g (8oz) self-raising flour
115g (4oz) vegetable suet
2 tbsp finely chopped flat-leaf parsley

**1** Preheat the oven to 160°C (325°F/Gas 3). Heat the oil in a large flameproof casserole over a medium heat, add the onion, and cook for 3–4 minutes until soft. Season with salt and pepper, then stir through the garlic and chilli flakes. Add the leek, carrots, and celery and continue cooking for a further 10 minutes, stirring occasionally, until softened. Stir in the plain flour, then gradually stir in the stock. Add the haricot beans and rosemary. Bring to the boil, then reduce to a simmer, cover, and put in the oven for 1 hour, checking on the liquid level as it cooks and topping up with hot stock if needed.

**2** While this is cooking, prepare the dumplings. Mix together the self-raising flour, suet, and parsley and season well. Add about 120ml (4fl oz) cold water to form a soft, slightly sticky dough, trickling in more water if it seems too dry. Form into 12 balls and drop them into the stew for the last 30 minutes of cooking. Push them down a little so they are just immersed and cover with the lid. Remove the lid for the final 10 minutes or until the dumplings are browned. Remove the rosemary, ladle the casserole into warmed bowls, and serve with crusty bread.

**SERVES** 4–6   **PREP** 25 MINS **COOK** 1¼ HOURS   **FREEZE** UP TO 1 MONTH

There is plenty of vibrant colour and a lot of heat in this vegetable dish. This is good on its own or with plain boiled rice and, to ring the changes, you may wish to add some chorizo or chicken.

# Jamaican corn stew

2 tbsp olive oil
2 onions, finely chopped
salt and freshly ground black pepper
3 garlic cloves, finely chopped
1 tsp cayenne pepper
3 sweetcorn cobs, cut into slices about
    1cm (½in) thick
2 red peppers, deseeded and roughly
    chopped
3 sweet potatoes, peeled and diced
175g (6oz) yellow split peas
300ml (10fl oz) hot vegetable stock
400ml can coconut milk
small handful of thyme
1 Scotch bonnet chilli, left whole

**1** Preheat the oven to 160°C (325°F/Gas 3). Heat the oil in a large flameproof casserole over a medium heat, add the onions, and cook for 3–4 minutes until soft. Season with salt and pepper, then stir through the garlic and cayenne pepper, and cook for 1 minute. Add the sweetcorn, peppers, and sweet potatoes and turn so it is all coated evenly. Then stir through the split peas and a little of the stock.

**2** Bring to the boil, then add the remaining stock and coconut milk. Bring back to the boil, reduce to a simmer, season, and add the thyme and the Scotch bonnet. Cover and put in the oven to cook for 1½–2 hours. Check occasionally that it's not drying out, topping up with a little hot water if needed.

**3** Remove the Scotch bonnet, taste, and season as required. Ladle into warmed bowls and serve with rice and some lime wedges on the side.

⊘ **SERVES** 4–6  🕐 **PREP** 20 MINS **COOK** 1½–2 HOURS

This is a vegetarian dish full of taste and texture with its fleshy aubergine and nutty chickpeas. It is an ideal dish to prepare a day ahead as the flavours become even better with time.

# Middle Eastern chickpea stew

2 tbsp olive oil
1 red onion, finely chopped
salt and freshly ground black pepper
½ tsp ground cinnamon
½ tsp ground cumin
½ tsp sumac (optional)
4 garlic cloves, finely chopped
1 large aubergine, roughly chopped into
   bite-sized pieces
150ml (5fl oz) white wine

2 x 400g cans chickpeas, drained and rinsed
400g can chopped tomatoes
1–2 tsp harissa paste, depending on how
   spicy you like it
60g (2oz) dried cherries or cranberries or
   use fresh pomegranate seeds
2 preserved lemons, quartered, flesh
   removed and discarded (optional)
900ml (1½ pints) hot vegetable stock
bunch of coriander leaves, chopped

**1** Heat the oil in a large heavy-based pan or tagine over a medium heat, add the onion, and cook for 3–4 minutes until soft. Season with salt and pepper, stir through the spices, garlic, and aubergine, and cook for 5–8 minutes, stirring, so it is all coated and the aubergine starts to turn golden brown.

**2** Add the wine and let it bubble for a minute, then add the chickpeas, tomatoes, harissa paste, cherries, and preserved lemons, if using. Stir well and pour in the stock. Bring to the boil, then reduce to a simmer, partially cover with the lid, and cook gently for 1 hour, stirring occasionally.

**3** Taste and season if needed, or stir through more harissa paste if you like it hot. Stir through most of the coriander and ladle into warmed shallow bowls, then sprinkle with the remaining coriander. Serve with warm flatbread and a spoonful of plain yogurt on the side.

**SERVES** 4–6    **PREP** 10 MINS **COOK** 1¼ HOURS    **FREEZE** UP TO 3 MONTHS

A medley of earthy mushrooms and potatoes makes this vegetarian dish a really hearty supper. Portabella mushrooms are especially meaty in texture so cut them into substantial chunks.

# Mixed mushroom stew

1 tbsp olive oil
1 onion, finely chopped
salt and freshly ground black pepper
175g (6oz) chestnut mushrooms, grated
450g (1lb) white mushrooms, thickly sliced
1 sprig of rosemary
3 garlic cloves, finely chopped
4 portabella mushrooms, roughly chopped
1 tbsp sherry vinegar

6 tomatoes, roughly chopped
1 tbsp tomato purée
450ml (15fl oz) hot vegetable stock)
3 potatoes, peeled and chopped into
   bite-sized pieces
pinch of dried chilli flakes
small bunch of curly parsley, finely chopped
25g (scant 1oz) Parmesan cheese,
   grated (optional)

**1** Heat the oil in a large heavy-based pan over a medium heat, add the onion, and cook for 3–4 minutes until soft. Season with salt and pepper, then add the grated chestnut mushrooms and cook for 5 minutes until they start to release their juices.

**2** Throw in the white mushrooms, rosemary, garlic, and portabella mushrooms, and stir. Add the sherry vinegar and allow the sauce to bubble for 1 minute, then add the tomatoes and tomato purée. Cook on a gentle heat for 5 minutes, stirring occasionally, then add the stock and bring to the boil. Reduce the heat to a simmer and cook, uncovered, on a low heat for 40–45 minutes.

**3** Stir through the potatoes for the last 20 minutes of cooking, and cook until tender. Taste and season as needed, remove the rosemary, then stir through the chilli flakes and parsley. Ladle into warmed bowls and serve with the grated Parmesan cheese, if using, and some chunky wholemeal bread.

⊙ **SERVES** 4–6     🕐 **PREP** 30 MINS **COOK** 1 HOUR     ❄ **FREEZE** UP TO 3 MONTHS

Puy lentils add texture to this dish as they hold their shape well when cooked. Add a little chilli heat, if you wish, and use butternut squash if pumpkin isn't available or out of season.

# Sweet and sour pumpkin stew

2 tbsp olive oil
1 onion, finely chopped
salt and freshly ground black pepper
3 garlic cloves, finely chopped
1 carrot, peeled and finely diced
2 celery sticks, finely diced
2 bay leaves
4 tbsp red wine vinegar
pinch of demerara sugar

1 pumpkin or large butternut squash, peeled and chopped into chunky pieces (about 500g/1lb 2oz prepared weight)
900ml (1½ pints) hot vegetable stock
150g (5½oz) Puy lentils, rinsed and picked over for any stones
bunch of mint leaves, roughly chopped
pumpkin seeds, to serve

**1** Heat the oil in a large flameproof casserole over a medium heat, add the onion, and cook for 3–4 minutes until soft. Season well with salt and pepper, then stir in the garlic, carrot, celery, and bay leaves, and cook for a further 5 minutes until soft.

**2** Increase the heat, add the vinegar, and let it bubble for a minute, then stir in the sugar and pumpkin. Turn to coat well and add a little stock before cooking on high for a minute. Stir through the lentils, add the remaining stock, and bring to the boil.

**3** Partially cover with the lid, reduce the heat, and simmer gently for about 45 minutes or until the lentils are soft. Top up with hot water if the stew is becoming to dry. Taste and season, if needed, and remove the bay leaf. Stir through the mint, then serve on a bed of rice with some pumpkin seeds scattered over.

**SERVES** 4    **PREP** 15 MINS **COOK** 1 HOUR    **FREEZE** UP TO 3 MONTHS

Pinto beans are creamy pink and, when mashed, are the common base filling of burritos. If you can't find them, use the same amount of black or kidney beans instead. They will taste just as good.

# Pinto bean chilli

1 tbsp olive oil
2 red onions, finely chopped
salt and freshly ground black pepper
3 garlic cloves, finely chopped
2–3 red chillies, depending on your heat
   preference, deseeded and finely chopped
1 tsp ground allspice
pinch of ground cumin
1 large cinnamon stick
1 tsp dried oregano
2 bay leaves
1 tbsp cider vinegar
2 x 400g cans chopped tomatoes
1 tbsp tomato purée
1 tbsp dark brown sugar
2 x 400g cans pinto beans,
   drained and rinsed
900ml (1½ pints) hot vegetable stock

**1** Heat the oil in a large heavy-based pan over a medium heat, add the onions, and cook for 3–4 minutes until soft. Season with salt and pepper, stir in the garlic, chillies, ground spices, and herbs, and cook for 2 minutes.

**2** Add the vinegar, tomatoes, tomato purée, sugar, beans, and stock and bring to the boil. Reduce to a simmer, partially cover with the lid, and cook gently for 1–1½ hours until thickened.

**3** Taste and season as needed, removing the bay leaves and cinnamon stick, and serve with bowls of grated cheese and soured cream, if you like.

⊘ **SERVES** 4–6     🕑 **PREP** 15 MINS **COOK** 1½ HOURS     ❄ **FREEZE** UP TO 3 MONTHS

This is a great vegetarian dish, with distinctively sweet flavours of cinnamon and cardamom. The peanuts add a contrasting texture to the potatoes and aubergine. Make it as hot and fiery as you wish.

# Aubergine massaman curry

2 red chillies, deseeded
1 lemongrass stalk, tough outer leaves removed
5cm (2in) piece of fresh root ginger, peeled and roughly chopped
5 cardamom pods, crushed
1 tbsp sunflower oil
1 onion, finely chopped
salt and freshly ground black pepper
600ml (1 pint) hot vegetable stock
400ml can coconut milk
1 cinnamon stick, broken

splash of dark soy sauce
splash of fish sauce (nam pla) – omit if cooking for vegetarians
4 potatoes, peeled and chopped into bite-sized pieces
6 baby aubergines, halved lengthways, or use 2 large ones, roughly chopped
1 tbsp palm sugar or demerara sugar (optional)
85g (3oz) roasted unsalted peanuts, roughly chopped

**1** Put the chillies, lemongrass, ginger, and cardamom in a food processor and whiz with a drop of the sunflower oil to make a paste.

**2** Heat the remaining oil in a large heavy-based pan over a medium heat, add the onion, and cook for 3–4 minutes until soft. Then add the paste and some seasoning and cook for a few minutes more. Stir in the stock and coconut milk, and bring to the boil, then add the cinnamon stick, soy sauce, and fish sauce, if using, and cook on a low heat for about 20 minutes. Stir in the potatoes and aubergines and cook for a further 20 minutes.

**3** Stir in half the peanuts, taste, and adjust the flavour by adding the sugar, if using, and more salt or fish sauce, also if using, as needed. Ladle into warmed bowls and sprinkle with the remaining peanuts. Serve with rice and lime wedges.

**SERVES** 4–6    **PREP** 15 MINS **COOK** 1 HOUR

This is a substantial vegetarian dish. The artichokes and butter beans give it a wonderful creamy finish and breadcrumbs are stirred through at the last minute to add some texture.

# Artichokes, butter beans, and peas

1 tbsp olive oil
1 onion, finely chopped
3 garlic cloves, finely chopped
250g (9oz) small button mushrooms, larger ones halved
200g (7oz) dried butter beans, soaked overnight and drained, or use 2 x 400g cans butter beans, drained and rinsed
pinch of ground nutmeg

juice of ½ lemon
salt and freshly ground black pepper
900ml (1½ pints) hot vegetable stock
125g (4½oz) frozen or fresh garden peas
675g (1½lb) antipasti artichoke hearts, drained
60g (2oz) breadcrumbs, toasted
few sprigs of flat-leaf parsley, finely chopped, to serve

**1** Heat the oil in a large heavy-based pan over a medium heat, add the onion, and cook for 3–4 minutes until soft. Then stir in the garlic and mushrooms and cook for about 5 minutes until the mushrooms are tender.

**2** Stir in the butter beans, add the nutmeg and lemon juice, and season with salt and pepper. Pour over the stock and bring to the boil. Boil for about 10 minutes, then reduce to a simmer, partially cover with the lid, and cook for 45 minutes. Check occasionally that it's not drying out, topping up with a little hot water if needed.

**3** Stir in the peas and artichokes and cook gently for a further 15–20 minutes or until the butter beans are completely soft. Spoon over the breadcrumbs and carefully fold some in, then top with the parsley. Serve with some freshly baked crusty bread.

**SERVES** 4–6 • **PREP** 15 MINS **COOK** 1½ HOURS • **FREEZE** UP TO 3 MONTHS

A colourful and gutsy dish, you could always add some spicy sausage or chorizo if you prefer a meaty meal. Black beans are also called turtle beans and need soaking overnight.

# Brazilian black bean and pumpkin stew

325g (11oz) dried black beans, soaked overnight and drained
1 tbsp olive oil
1 onion, finely chopped
salt and freshly ground black pepper
3 garlic cloves, finely chopped
1 small pumpkin or butternut squash, peeled, deseeded, and diced

2 red peppers, deseeded and diced
2 x 400g cans chopped tomatoes
1 small green chilli, deseeded and diced
900ml (1½ pint) hot vegetable stock
1 mango, peeled, stone removed, and diced
bunch of coriander, chopped

**1** Preheat the oven to 160°C (325°F/Gas 3). Put the beans in a large heavy-based pan and cover with water. Bring to the boil, then reduce to a simmer, partially cover with the lid, and cook on a low heat for 1 hour. Drain and set aside.

**2** Heat the oil in a large heavy-based pan over a medium heat, add the onion, and cook for 3–4 minutes until soft. Season with salt and pepper, stir in the garlic, and cook for 1–2 minutes until soft. Stir in the pumpkin or butternut squash, red peppers, tomatoes, and chilli.

**3** Add the beans, pour over the stock, and bring to the boil. Then reduce to a simmer, cover with the lid and put in the oven for 1½–2 hours. Taste and season, if necessary, then stir through the mango and coriander. Serve with some soured cream and rice on the side.

**SERVES** 4–6      **PREP** 25 MINS, PLUS SOAKING      **FREEZE** UP TO 3 MONTHS
**COOK** 2½–3 HOURS

This is a mild vegetarian curry and the sweet peppers marry well with the paneer. This is an Indian cheese that won't melt upon cooking; you'll find it with the other cheeses at the supermarket.

# Paneer and sweet pepper curry

2 tbsp vegetable oil
1 x 230g packet paneer, cubed
10cm (4in) piece fresh root ginger,
    peeled and sliced
2 red chillies, deseeded and
    finely chopped
2 tbsp dried curry leaves, crushed
2 tsp cumin seeds
4 tsp garam masala
2 tsp ground turmeric
6 red peppers, deseeded and sliced
6 tomatoes, skinned and roughly chopped
salt and freshly ground black pepper
bunch of coriander, finely chopped

**1** Heat half the oil in a heavy-based pan over a medium-high heat, add the paneer and cook for 5–8 minutes, stirring, until golden all over. Remove and set aside.

**2** Heat the remaining oil in the pan, add the ginger, chillies, curry leaves, cumin seeds, garam masala, and turmeric, and stir well to coat with the oil. Then add the peppers and cook over a low heat for about 15 minutes until beginning to soften.

**3** Add the tomatoes and 100ml (3½fl oz) water and cook on low for 15 minutes. Return the paneer to the pan, season with salt and pepper, then simmer gently for 15–20 minutes, topping up with a little hot water if needed. Stir through the coriander and serve with rice, chapatis, or naan bread.

🍲 **SERVES** 4–6     🕐 **PREP** 20 MINS **COOK** 1 HOUR

Lots of spices enliven these red lentils, making them delicious enough to eat on their own with rice. Wash the lentils well before using and pick them over for any stones.

# Red lentil dahl

1 tbsp sunflower oil
1 onion, finely chopped
salt and freshly ground black pepper
3 garlic cloves, finely chopped
1 red chilli, deseeded and finely chopped
5cm (2in) piece of fresh root ginger,
   peeled and grated
1 tsp ground cumin
1 tsp ground coriander
1 tsp ground turmeric

1 tsp paprika
6 curry leaves, crushed
175g (6oz) red lentils, rinsed and
   picked over for any stones
400g can chopped tomatoes
900ml (1½ pints) hot vegetable stock
juice of ½ lemon (optional)
small bunch of coriander leaves,
   finely chopped

**1** Heat the oil in a large heavy-based pan over a medium heat, add the onion, and cook for 3–4 minutes until soft. Season with salt and pepper, stir through the garlic, chilli, and ginger, and cook for a couple more minutes.

**2** Add all the spices and curry leaves and stir well, then stir through the lentils so they are well coated with the spices. Tip in the tomatoes and 600ml (1 pint) of the stock. Bring to the boil, then reduce to a simmer, partially cover with the lid, and cook on a low heat for about 1 hour, stirring occasionally and topping up with the reserved stock when needed.

**3** Taste and season as needed, adding the lemon juice, if using, and stir through the coriander. Serve with rice, chapatis, and a spoonful of yogurt on the side.

**SERVES** 4    **PREP** 15 MINS **COOK** 1¼ HOURS    **FREEZE** UP TO 3 MONTHS

One of the ingredients that gives a Moroccan tagine its unique flavour is preserved lemon. The lemons are pickled in salt water with lemon juice and are available at large supermarkets.

# Mixed vegetable tagine

1 tbsp olive oil
1 red onion, roughly chopped
salt and freshly ground black pepper
3 garlic cloves, finely chopped
5cm (2in) piece of fresh root ginger, peeled and grated
1 tsp ground turmeric
pinch of saffron threads
1 tsp coriander seeds, ground
½ tsp cumin seeds
4 large potatoes, peeled and chopped into chunky pieces

3 carrots, peeled and chopped into chunky pieces
1 fennel bulb, trimmed and chopped into chunky pieces
4 tomatoes, finely chopped
about 750ml (1¼ pints) hot vegetable stock
handful of mixed olives, stoned and halved (optional)
2 preserved lemons, halved, flesh discarded and peel chopped (optional)
bunch of coriander leaves, roughly chopped

**1** Heat the oil in a large heavy-based pan or tagine over a medium heat, add the onion, and cook for 3–4 minutes until soft. Season with salt and pepper, stir through the garlic, ginger, turmeric, saffron, coriander seeds, and cumin, and cook for a couple of minutes.

**2** Add the potatoes and toss to coat, then add the carrots and fennel and stir so everything is well combined. Cook for a few minutes, add the tomatoes, and pour over just enough stock to cover the vegetables.

**3** Cover with the lid and simmer very gently for 30–40 minutes until the vegetables are soft and a lot of the liquid has evaporated. Top up with more hot stock if needed. Taste and season, then stir through the olives and lemon, if using, and half the coriander leaves. Transfer to a serving dish and sprinkle over the remaining coriander leaves. Serve with couscous.

**SERVES** 4–6　　**PREP** 25–25 MINS **COOK** 50 MINS　　**FREEZE** UP TO 3 MONTHS

Except for squid, seafood doesn't take kindly to stewing, so make the stew base first and add the fish at the last minute. For ease of preparation, you could always make this the day before.

# Seafood stew

2 tbsp olive oil, plus extra for drizzling
1 onion, finely chopped
2 celery sticks, finely chopped
salt and freshly ground black pepper
1 tbsp dried oregano
1 fennel bulb, trimmed and roughly chopped
450g (1lb) cleaned squid, sliced
    into 1cm (½in) rings
350ml (12fl oz) dry white wine
2 lemons, zest peeled into strips using
    a vegetable peeler
1 tbsp tomato purée

400g can chopped tomatoes
900ml (1½ pints) hot fish stock
1kg (2¼lb) mussels, scrubbed and
    debearded (discard any that do
    not close when tapped)
250g (9oz) raw shelled king prawns
350g (12oz) sea bass fillet (or other
    white fish such as haddock), skinned
    and cut into chunky pieces
few sprigs of flat-leaf parsley,
    finely chopped

**1** Preheat the oven to 160°C (325°F/Gas 3). Heat the oil in a large flameproof casserole over a medium heat, add the onion and celery, and cook for about 5 minutes until soft. Season with salt and pepper, then stir in the oregano and fennel and cook for a further 5 minutes.

**2** Add the squid and cook over a low heat for a few minutes, stirring occasionally, then stir in the wine, and bring to the boil for 5 minutes. Stir in the strips of lemon zest and tomato purée, season well, and then add the canned tomatoes and stock. Bring back to the boil, reduce to a simmer, cover, and put in the oven for 1 hour, topping up with hot stock if needed.

**3** Add the mussels, prawns, and sea bass to the casserole, cover with the lid once more, and put back in the oven for 5 minutes or until the mussels have opened (discard any that do not open) and the fish is opaque and cooked through. Taste and season as needed. Ladle into deep, warmed bowls and serve with rice, couscous, or quinoa, a drizzle of olive oil, and a sprinkling of parsley.

⊘ **SERVES** 4–6    🕒 **PREP** 20–30 MINS **COOK** 1½ HOURS

The basis of this tasty stew is sweetcorn. If you can't get hold of creamed sweetcorn, use a can of regular sweetcorn and blend it in the food processor. Omit the fish if you are cooking for vegetarians

# Creole fish and corn stew

2 tbsp olive oil
1 onion, finely chopped
3 garlic cloves, finely chopped
3 celery sticks, finely chopped
3 carrots, peeled and finely chopped
1 tsp dried oregano
few sprigs of thyme, leaves only
1 tsp cayenne pepper (use less if
   you don't like it too hot)
400g can creamed sweetcorn

400g can sweetcorn, drained
900ml (1½ pints) hot vegetable stock
salt and freshly ground black pepper
2 potatoes, peeled and diced into
   bite-sized pieces
200g (7oz) ready-cooked prawns, chopped
300g (10oz) white fish, skinned and
   cut into chunky pieces
splash of Tabasco sauce (optional)

**1** Heat the oil in a large heavy-based pan over a medium heat, add the onion, and cook for 3–4 minutes until soft. Then stir through the garlic, celery, and carrot and cook on a gentle heat for a further 5 minutes or until the carrot is soft.

**2** Stir through the herbs and cayenne pepper, then add both the cans of sweetcorn and the stock. Season well with salt and pepper, bring to the boil, reduce to a simmer and cook gently, partially covered, for 30–40 minutes. Add the potatoes and cook for a further 15 minutes.

**3** Add the prawns and fish to the casserole and simmer gently for 6–10 minutes, until the fish is opaque and cooked through. Taste and season further, if necessary, and stir in the Tabasco sauce, if using. Ladle into warmed bowls and serve with crusty bread.

**SERVES** 4–6   **PREP** 15 MINS **COOK** 1¼ HOURS   **FREEZE** UP TO 1 MONTH

In this dish, salt cod is tender and fragrant with the classic Spanish aromas of garlic, bay leaves, and saffron. If you can't get salt cod, use a white fish and add it in for the last 15 minutes of cooking.

# Salt cod braised with vegetables

800g (1¾lb) thick-cut salt cod, or
   fresh white fish such as sustainable
   cod, haddock, or halibut
3 tbsp olive oil
1 onion, finely diced
2 leeks, trimmed and white
   parts finely sliced
3 garlic cloves, finely chopped

3 tomatoes, skinned and chopped
500g (1lb 2oz) potatoes, diced
salt and freshly ground black pepper
2 bay leaves
large pinch of saffron threads
120ml (4fl oz) dry white wine
2 tbsp chopped parsley, to serve

**1** If using the salt cod, soak the pieces of cod in enough cold water to cover them for at least 24 hours, changing the water 2–3 times to remove the saltiness of the brine. Drain and cut the fish into 4 pieces, then pat dry with kitchen paper. If using the fresh fish, simply cut the fish into 4 pieces.

**2** Heat the oil in a large heavy-based pan over a medium heat, add the onion and leeks, and cook for about 5 minutes until soft. Add the garlic and tomatoes and cook for a further 2 minutes, stirring. Add the potatoes, seasoning, bay leaves, and saffron.

**3** Pour in the wine and 250ml (9fl oz) water and sit the cod, skin-side up, on top of the vegetables. Bring gently to a simmer and cook for 25–30 minutes until the fish is opaque and cooked through. Shake the pan once or twice every 5 minutes to help release gelatine from the fish, to thicken the sauce. Ladle into warmed bowls, sprinkle with the parsley, and serve with a crisp mixed salad and some crusty bread.

**SERVES** 4    **PREP** 20 MINS, PLUS SOAKING **COOK** 40 MINS

This is a classic one-pot French dish in which chicken is simmered until the meat falls off the bone. If you can use a fresh chicken stock for this, all the better.

# Chicken fricassée

2 tbsp olive oil
4 chicken legs, divided into drumstick
   and thigh joints, skin removed
2 tbsp plain flour, seasoned with salt
   and pepper
4 shallots, sliced
2 garlic cloves, crushed
115g (4oz) button mushrooms, sliced
4 waxy potatoes, peeled and chopped
   into small pieces
2 tsp finely chopped rosemary leaves
150ml (5fl oz) dry white wine
300ml (10fl oz) hot chicken stock
1 bay leaf
salt and freshly ground black pepper

**1** Heat the oil in a large flameproof casserole over a medium heat. Toss the chicken pieces in the flour and then cook for 8–10 minutes, turning often, until golden brown. Remove and set aside.

**2** Add the shallots to the casserole and cook for 2–3 minutes, stirring often. Stir in the garlic, mushrooms, potatoes, and rosemary and also cook for 2 minutes.

**3** Pour in the wine and bring to the boil, then allow it to simmer and reduce for 1 minute. Pour in the stock, and bring to the boil. Return the chicken to the casserole, add the bay leaf, and cover tightly. Reduce the heat and cook gently for 45 minutes or until the chicken is very tender. Discard the bay leaf and adjust the seasoning, if needed. Serve hot with courgettes or sautéed cabbage.

**SERVES** 4   **PREP** 15 MINS **COOK** 1 HOUR   **FREEZE** UP TO 3 MONTHS

In Italy, this dish is called *alla cacciatora,* meaning "hunter's style". Chicory, with its slight bitterness, makes a flavoursome addition and must be added towards the end of cooking.

# Hunter's chicken stew

1.5kg (3lb 3oz) chicken, jointed
   into 8 pieces
salt and freshly ground black pepper
4 tbsp olive oil
1 onion, chopped
4 garlic cloves, finely chopped
1 sprig of rosemary
1 bay leaf
4 tbsp dry white wine
120ml (4fl oz) hot chicken stock
2 heads of chicory (also known as
   Belgian endive), trimmed, leaves
   separated, and roughly chopped

**1** Season the chicken all over with salt and pepper. Heat half the oil in a large flameproof casserole over a medium heat, add the thighs and drumsticks, skin-side down, and cook for about 5 minutes until they begin to brown. Add the breast pieces and cook gently for 10–15 minutes until very brown. Turn and brown the other side. Lower the heat.

**2** Add the onion and garlic, stir, and continue cooking gently for 3–4 minutes until they are soft. Season with salt and pepper, then stir in the rosemary, bay leaf, wine, and stock. Cover and simmer for 15–20 minutes until tender.

**3** Add the chicory for the last 5 minutes of cooking, return the lid, and cook gently until it has just softened. Discard the bay leaf and rosemary from the sauce, taste, and add seasoning if needed. Spoon out into warmed bowls and serve with crusty bread.

**SERVES** 4    **PREP** 20–25 MINS **COOK** 45–60 MINS    **FREEZE** UP TO 3 MONTHS,
WITHOUT THE CHICORY

Chicken and mustard is a classic combination – and in this recipe mustard is mixed with honey for a sweet marinade. If you have the time, let the chicken marinate for a few hours.

# Mustard chicken casserole

2 tbsp wholegrain mustard
1 tbsp English mustard
2 tbsp runny honey
8 chicken thighs, skin on
salt and freshly ground black pepper
2 tbsp olive oil
2 onions, roughly chopped
300g (10oz) parsnips, peeled and
    roughly chopped
few sprigs of thyme
900ml (1½ pints) hot vegetable or
    chicken stock
bunch of flat-leaf parsley, finely chopped

**1** Preheat the oven to 160°C (325°F/Gas 3). Mix together the mustards in a bowl and stir through the honey. Season the chicken thighs well with salt and pepper, then smother them with the mustard mixture. Cover and leave to marinate for 30 minutes, if time permits.

**2** Heat half the oil in a large flameproof casserole over a medium-high heat and add the chicken pieces, a few at a time. Cook for 6–10 minutes until golden – be careful, as the honey may cause them to blacken quickly. Remove and set aside.

**3** Heat the remaining oil in the casserole over a medium heat, add the onions, and toss them around the casserole to coat in any juices. Stir to scrape up the sticky bits from the bottom, then add the parsnips and thyme. Pour in the stock, bring to the boil, and then reduce to a simmer. Return the chicken pieces to the casserole together with any juices, nestling them in between the parsnips and making sure they are covered in liquid. Season, cover, and put in the oven for 1½ hours. Check occasionally that it's not drying out, topping up with a little hot water if needed. Add the parsley, taste, and season, if necessary. Serve with steamed leeks or greens.

 **SERVES** 4–6    **PREP** 10–25 MINS, PLUS MARINATING    **FREEZE** UP TO 1 MONTH
**COOK** 1¾ HOURS

This is a relatively dry curry, although if you like a curry with more sauce, you can top up the stock during cooking. Fresh ginger and bird's eye chillies make the dish more fragrant.

# Karahi chicken

1 tsp coriander seeds
2 green chillies, deseeded
3 garlic cloves, peeled
1 tsp ground turmeric
2 tbsp sunflower oil
8 chicken thighs, skin on, slashed a
  few times across each thigh
salt and freshly ground black pepper

1 onion, roughly chopped
6 tomatoes, roughly chopped
900ml (1½ pints) hot vegetable stock
5cm (2in) piece of fresh root ginger,
  peeled and finely chopped
3–4 green bird's eye chillies, left whole
bunch of coriander, finely chopped

**1** Put the coriander seeds, chillies, garlic, turmeric, and half the oil into a food processor and blend until it becomes a paste. Season the chicken with salt and pepper and smother them with the paste, using your hands and pushing it into all the cuts. Heat half the remaining oil in a large flameproof casserole over a medium-high heat and add the chicken pieces. Cook for 5–6 minutes on each side or until beginning to colour, then remove and set aside.

**2** Heat the remaining oil in the casserole over a medium heat, add the onion, and cook for 3–4 minutes until soft. Then add the tomatoes and cook for a further 5–10 minutes until they, too, are soft. Pour in the stock and bring to the boil. Reduce to a simmer, stir in the ginger and bird's eye chillies, and return the chicken to the casserole. Cover with the lid and cook gently for 30–40 minutes, keeping an eye on the sauce. You want it to be fairly dry, but it is sticking, add a little hot water.

**3** Remove the chillies, then taste and season, as necessary, stirring through the coriander. Serve with rice, chapatis, and some minted yogurt on the side.

⚙ **SERVES** 4     🕐 **PREP** 15 MINS **COOK** 1 HOUR     ❄ **FREEZE** UP TO 1 MONTH

This dish is slow cooked in a casserole, but you could always use a tagine if you have one. Preserved lemons have a subtle and distinctive flavour and are available at larger supermarkets.

# Chicken and green olive tagine

4 tbsp olive oil
1 tbsp ground ginger
2 tbsp paprika
pinch of cayenne pepper
1 tsp ground turmeric
salt and freshly ground black pepper
8 chicken drumsticks
4 onions, roughly chopped
4 garlic cloves, finely chopped
pinch of saffron threads
2.5cm (1in) piece of fresh root ginger,
    peeled and grated

4 large tomatoes, roughly chopped
juice of 1 lemon
900ml (1½ pints) hot vegetable stock
150g (5½oz) green olives in brine,
    stoned and rinsed
2 preserved lemons, halved, flesh
    discarded, and rind shredded (optional)
handful of coriander, chopped
handful of flat-leaf parsley, chopped

**1** In a bowl, mix together half the oil with the spices and season with salt and pepper. Add the chicken drumsticks and toss until they are really well coated. Cover and leave overnight in the fridge, if time allows, or leave for 30 minutes. Preheat the oven to 190°C (375°F/Gas 5). Heat a large flameproof casserole or tagine, add the chicken drumsticks (in batches and with extra oil, if necessary), and cook for 6–8 minutes until golden. Remove from the casserole and set aside.

**2** Heat 1 tbsp of the oil in the casserole, add the onion, and cook for 3–4 minutes until soft. Then stir through the garlic, grated ginger, and saffron and cook for a minute more. Stir in the tomatoes and return the chicken to the casserole with any juices and the lemon juice. Season and pour in the stock. Bring to the boil, then reduce to a simmer, cover, and put in the oven for 1 hour. Add the olives and preserved lemons, if using, and cook for 30 minutes more. Check occasionally that it's not drying out, topping up with a little hot water if needed. Sprinkle over the herbs and serve with couscous.

**SERVES** 4–6    **PREP** 20 MINS, PLUS MARINATING    **FREEZE** UP TO 1 MONTH
**COOK** 2 HOURS

The darker the beer, the richer this dish will be. Cognac is also added, to add depth of flavour. Mashed potatoes would be good with it and, naturally, you can guess what is the best drink to serv

# Chicken and beer stew

4 chicken breasts on the bone
salt and freshly ground black pepper
30g (1oz) butter
2 tbsp vegetable oil
750g (1lb 10oz) onions, thinly sliced
30g (1oz) plain flour
3–4 tbsp Cognac
500g (1lb 2oz) mushrooms, quartered

1 bouquet garni, made with 5–6 parsley
    sprigs, 2–3 thyme sprigs, and 1 bay leaf
2 tsp juniper berries, gently crushed
500ml (16fl oz) beer
250ml (9fl oz) hot chicken stock
4 tbsp double cream
small bunch of flat-leaf parsley,
    leaves finely chopped

**1** Season the chicken pieces. Heat the butter and oil in a large flameproof casserole over a medium-high heat until foaming. Add the chicken, skin-side down (in batches, if necessary) and cook for about 5 minutes on each side until browned. Remove and set aside.

**2** Reduce the heat to medium, add the onions, and cook for about 10 minutes until soft and well browned. Sprinkle with the flour and cook, stirring, for 1–2 minutes until the flour is just lightly browned. Return the chicken to the casserole in a single layer. Add the Cognac and bring to the boil for a few minutes, basting the chicken with the Cognac. Add the mushrooms, bouquet garni, and crushed juniper berries. Pour in the beer and stock, bring to the boil, cover with the lid, and simmer for 40–50 minutes until the chicken is tender when pierced and the juices run clear.

**3** Discard the bouquet garni and skim off excess fat from the surface. Stir in the cream for the last 15 minutes of cooking. Taste, and add seasoning if needed. Sprinkle with the parsley and serve.

**SERVES** 4–6     **PREP** 15 MINS **COOK** 1 HOUR     **FREEZE** UP TO 3 MONTHS

In Mexico, chorizo is made with fresh pork, but in Spain, the pork is smoked first for even more flavour. Chorizo works its magic as it cooks and gives the sauce a rich, deep flavour.

# Chicken with chorizo

2 tbsp olive oil
4 skinless chicken legs
250g (9oz) chorizo, chopped into
  bite-sized pieces
1 red onion, thinly sliced
1 tsp ground coriander
1 tsp chopped thyme leaves
1 red pepper, deseeded and chopped
1 yellow pepper, deseeded and chopped
1 courgette, trimmed and sliced
2 garlic cloves, crushed
400g can chopped tomatoes
200ml (7fl oz) hot chicken stock
60ml (2fl oz) dry sherry
freshly ground black pepper

**1** Preheat the oven to 180°C (350°F/Gas 4). Heat the oil in a large flameproof casserole over a medium-high heat, add the chicken, and fry for 5–8 minutes, turning frequently, until evenly browned. Remove and set aside. Then add the chorizo to the casserole and cook for 2–3 minutes until lightly browned, stirring frequently. Also remove and set aside.

**2** Reduce the heat to medium, add the onion to the casserole, and cook for 3–4 minutes until soft. Add the coriander, cook for 1 minute, and then add the thyme, peppers, courgette, and garlic and cook for 5 minutes. Add the tomatoes, stock, and sherry. Season with black pepper, if needed, and bring to the boil. Return the chicken and chorizo, and cook in the oven for about 40 minutes until the chicken is tender when pierced with a fork. Serve with mashed sweet potatoes and peas.

⊘ **SERVES** 4     🕐 **PREP** 10 MINS **COOK** 1 HOUR     ❄ **FREEZE** UP TO 1 MONTH

Duck curry is extremely rich and has a great depth of flavour. If you like your curry hot, use two red chillies rather than the one specified – and leave the seeds in for an even greater kick.

# Duck curry

2 duck breasts
1 tbsp sunflower oil
1 onion, finely chopped
2 celery sticks, finely chopped
salt and freshly ground black pepper
3 garlic cloves, finely chopped
1 red chilli, deseeded and finely chopped
5cm (2in) piece of fresh root ginger,
    peeled and finely chopped

2 carrots, peeled and finely chopped
1 tbsp garam masala
1 tsp ground turmeric
1 tsp paprika
1 tbsp tomato purée
2 x 400g cans chopped tomatoes
900ml (1½ pint) hot vegetable stock

**1** Preheat the oven to 180°C (350°F/Gas 4). Heat a large flameproof casserole over a medium-high heat and add the duck breasts, skin-side down. Cook each side for 3–6 minutes or until golden. Remove and set aside. Heat the oil in the casserole over a medium heat, add the onion and celery, and cook for about 5 minutes until soft. Season with salt and pepper, stir in the garlic, chilli, and ginger, and cook for a couple more minute

**2** Add the carrots, turn to coat, and continue cooking for 5 more minutes, stirring occasionally. Stir through the spices and tomato purée and cook for 1–2 minutes, then tip in the tomatoes and stock. Bring to the boil, reduce to a simmer, and return the duck breasts to the casserole, tucking them into the sauce. Cover with the lid and put in the oven for 1½ hours. Check occasionally that it's not drying out, topping up with a little hot water if needed.

**3** Remove from the oven and spoon out the duck breasts. Peel off the skin and then shred the meat. Put the duck meat back into the casserole and return it to the oven for another 30 minutes (if the sauce is too thin, remove the lid). Taste and season, if necessary. Serve with rice and chapatis.

⊘ **SERVES** 4    🕐 **PREP** 15 MINS **COOK** 2 HOURS    ❄ **FREEZE** UP TO 1 MONTH

This stew is a favourite dish in northern Italy. Barbera is the preferred wine, but substitute any good-quality dry red; you will taste a bad wine if you use it in a dish.

# Italian beef braised in red wine

2 tbsp olive oil
1kg (2¼lb) stewing beef, cut into
  bite-sized pieces
1 small onion, finely chopped
1 small carrot, peeled and finely chopped
1 celery stick, finely chopped
500ml (16fl oz) dry red wine
2 tbsp tomato purée
about 500ml (16fl oz) hot beef stock
2–3 thyme sprigs
salt and freshly ground black pepper

**1** Preheat the oven to 150°C (300°F/Gas 2). Heat the oil in a large flameproof casserole over a medium-high heat, add the beef (in batches, if necessary) and cook for about 10 minutes until browned on all sides. Remove from the casserole and set aside. Add the onion, carrot, and celery, and cook, stirring, for 3–5 minutes until the vegetables are soft.

**2** Add the red wine, stir to dissolve the casserole juices, and bring to the boil. Stir in the tomato purée and return the beef. Add enough stock to cover the meat, add the thyme and seasoning, and bring to the boil. Cover with the lid and put in the oven to cook for 2–3 hours or until the meat is very tender when pierced with a fork. Check occasionally that it's not drying out, topping up with a little hot water if needed. Discard the thyme, taste, and add seasoning if needed. Ladle into shallow bowls and serve with some crusty bread.

**SERVES** 6   **PREP** 15 MINS **COOK** 2¼–3¼ HOURS   **FREEZE** UP TO 3 MONTHS

The all-important ingredient in a carbonnade – a classic Belgian casserole – is the beer. Here it is topped with slices of French bread and mustard, which soak into the pot and enhance the gravy.

# Beef carbonnade

knob of butter
2 tbsp olive oil
1.1kg (2½lb) skirt beef, cut into chunks
1–2 tbsp plain flour, seasoned with
  salt and pepper
12 baby shallots, peeled and left whole
salt and freshly ground black pepper
3 garlic cloves, finely chopped
1 tbsp demerara sugar

300ml (10fl oz) Belgian beer or
  dark brown ale
pinch of grated nutmeg
1 bouquet garni
900ml, 1½ pints hot beef stock
1 tbsp Dijon mustard
1 small French stick, cut into slices
handful of flat-leaf parsley, finely chopped

**1** Preheat the oven to 160°C (325°F/Gas 3). Heat the butter and 1 tbsp of the oil in a large flameproof casserole over a medium-high heat. Toss the meat in the flour, and cook in batches for about 10 minutes until golden. Remove and set aside. Reduce the temperature, add the remaining oil, and cook the shallots for 8–10 minutes, stirring so they don't burn. Add seasoning, garlic, and sugar, and cook for a few minutes, adding more oil if needed. Remove and set aside.

**2** Increase the heat, add the beer, and let it boil for a few minutes. Then reduce the heat, return the meat and shallot mixture to the casserole, and add the nutmeg and bouquet garni. Pour over the stock, cover with the lid, and put the casserole in the oven for 2 hours or until the beef is meltingly tender. Check occasionally that it's not drying out, topping up with a little hot water if needed.

**3** Spread the mustard over the slices of French bread and place on top of the stew. Cover with the lid and return to the oven for 30 minutes. Uncover and give the topping about 10 minutes to brown. Remove the bouquet garni and sprinkle with parsley. Ladle into warmed large shallow bowls to serve.

**SERVES** 4–6  **PREP** 10 MINS **COOK** 3¼ HOURS  **FREEZE** UP TO 3 MONTHS

Tender beef with robust kale is a great combination. The chilli hint is subtle, but just enough to add interest to the dish, while the anchovies are added to enrich the sauce.

# Beef and greens

3–4 tbsp olive oil
1.25kg (2¾lb) chuck beef, cut into
   bite-sized pieces
salt and freshly ground black pepper
1 tsp paprika
1 tbsp plain flour
2 onions, roughly chopped
3 garlic cloves, finely chopped
1 green chilli, deseeded and finely chopped
8 salted anchovies
4 large carrots, peeled and roughly chopped
250ml (9fl oz) red wine
900ml (1½ pint) hot beef or vegetable stock
4 large potatoes, peeled and roughly chopped
200g pack curly kale, stems trimmed and
   leaves roughly chopped

**1** Preheat the oven to 160°C (325°F/Gas 3). Heat 1 tbsp of the oil in a large flameproof casserole over a medium heat. Season the meat with salt, pepper, and paprika, then toss in the flour. Add the beef to the casserole (in batches and with extra oil, if necessary), and cook for 5–8 minutes until browned all over. Remove with a slotted spoon and set aside.

**2** Add the remaining oil to the casserole, add the onions, and cook for 3–4 minutes until soft Then stir in the garlic, chilli, and anchovies and cook for a minute. Add the carrots and cook for a further 2–3 minutes.

**3** Pour in the wine and bring to the boil, stirring and scraping up the bits from the bottom o the casserole. Pour in the stock and bring back to the boil, add the meat and potatoes, cover and put in the oven for 1½ hours. Check occasionally that it's not drying out, topping up wit a little hot water if needed. Add the kale and cook for a further hour, again checking that it doesn't dry out too much. Serve while piping hot with some crusty bread.

 **SERVES** 4–6   **PREP** 15 MINS **COOK** 1¾ HOURS   ❄ **FREEZE** UP TO 3 MONTHS

This beef is cooked slowly in sweet Madeira for maximum flavour. Buy the meat in one piece from your butcher and don't forget to soak the dried porcini mushrooms in water for 20 minutes.

# Beef pot roast

2 tbsp olive oil
900g (2lb) whole piece of chuck beef
salt and freshly ground black pepper
1 large onion, chopped into eighths
1 tbsp wholegrain mustard
150ml (5fl oz) Madeira wine
30g (1oz) dried porcini mushrooms, soaked
   in 120ml (4fl oz) warm water for 20 mins,
   strained, and liquid reserved
900ml (1½ pint) hot beef stock
handful of flat-leaf parsley, finely chopped

**1** Preheat the oven to 160°C (325°F/Gas 3). Heat half the oil in a large flameproof casserole over a medium-high heat. Season the beef with salt and pepper, add it to the casserole, and cook for 6–8 minutes on each side until golden. It is ready when it lifts away from the bottom of the casserole easily. Remove and set aside.

**2** Heat the remaining oil in the casserole over a medium heat, add the onion, and cook for 3–4 minutes until soft. Stir through the mustard, increase the heat, and add the Madeira wine. Cook for a minute, then add the drained mushrooms, beef stock, and about 100ml (3½fl oz) of the strained mushroom liquid. Bring to the boil and stir, then reduce to a simmer and return the beef to the casserole.

**3** Cover with the lid and put in the oven for 2 hours. Check occasionally that it's not drying out, topping up with a little hot water if needed. Be careful not to add too much, however, or this will dilute the flavour. Taste and season as necessary. Sprinkle with parsley and serve with mashed potatoes or baby cubed roast potatoes.

**SERVES** 4–6    **PREP** 10 MINS, PLUS SOAKING **COOK** 2½ HOURS    **FREEZE** UP TO 1 MONTH

This Italian classic is served with a zesty gremolata, and it would be delicious with a saffron and Parmesan risotto. Ask your butcher for a hindleg of veal as they are meatier than the front legs.

# Osso bucco

30g (1oz) plain flour
salt and freshly ground black pepper
4–6 pieces of veal shin on the bone
    (about 1.8kg/4lb)
2 tbsp vegetable oil
30g (1oz) butter
1 carrot, peeled and thinly sliced
2 onions, finely chopped
250ml (9fl oz) white wine
400g can Italian plum tomatoes,
    drained and coarsely chopped

1 garlic clove, finely chopped
finely grated zest of 1 orange
120ml (4fl oz) hot chicken
    or veal stock

**For the gremolata**
small bunch of flat-leaf parsley,
    leaves finely chopped
finely grated zest of 1 lemon
1 garlic clove, finely chopped

**1** Preheat the oven to 180°C (350°F/Gas 4). Put the flour on a large plate, season with salt and pepper, and stir to combine. Lightly coat the veal pieces with the seasoned flour. Heat the oil and butter in a large flameproof casserole over a medium heat, add the veal pieces (in batches and with extra oil, if necessary), and brown thoroughly on all sides. Transfer to a plate with a slotted spoon and set aside.

**2** Add the carrot and onions and cook, stirring occasionally, until soft. Add the wine and boil until reduced by half. Stir in the tomatoes, garlic, and orange zest, and add seasoning. Transfer everything to the slow cooker, then lay the veal on top, and pour over the stock. Cover with the lid and put in the oven for 1½–2 hours until very tender. Check occasionally that it's not drying out, topping up with a little hot water if needed.

**3** For the gremolata, mix the parsley, lemon, and garlic in a small bowl. Put the veal on warmed plates, spoon the sauce on top and sprinkle with the gremolata.

**SERVES** 4–6    **PREP** 30–35 MINS **COOK** 1¾–2¼ HOURS    **FREEZE** UP TO 3 MONTHS

The vivid flavours of young lamb and baby vegetables marry perfectly in this springtime stew. Cook the lamb until it is soft enough to fall from a fork, while only lightly cooking the vegetable

# Navarin of lamb

2 tbsp vegetable oil
500g (1lb 2oz) baby onions, peeled and left whole
750g (1lb 10oz) boneless lamb shoulder, cut into bite-sized pieces
2 tbsp plain flour, seasoned with salt and pepper
1 tbsp tomato purée
2 garlic cloves, finely chopped
1 bouquet garni made with 5–6 parsley sprigs, 2–3 thyme sprigs, and 1 bay leaf
about 750ml/1¼ pints hot chicken or lamb stock

750g (1lb 10oz) small new potatoes, peeled or scrubbed
250g (9oz) turnips, peeled and quartered
375g (13oz) tomatoes, skinned, deseeded, and coarsely chopped
250g (9oz) baby carrots, topped and small ones left whole or halved
150g (5½oz) fresh or frozen peas (optional)
250g (9oz) French beans, topped and chopped into 2.5cm (1in) pieces
salt and freshly ground black pepper
few sprigs of flat-leaf parsley, leaves chopped

**1** Heat the oil in a large flameproof casserole over a medium heat, add the baby onions, and cook for 5–7 minutes until golden. Remove and set aside. Toss the lamb in the flour and cook (in batches, if necessary) for 5–8 minutes over a high heat until browned. Stir in the tomato purée, garlic, and bouquet garni, pour in enough stock to just cover, and bring to the boil. Cover with the lid and simmer for 1 hour.

**2** Add the baby onions, potatoes, turnips, tomatoes, and carrots. Pour in more stock to almost cover the meat and vegetables. Cover and simmer for 20–25 minutes until the potatoes are tender to the point of a knife. Add the peas, if using, and beans and simmer until they are just tender. Be sure not to cook the navarin for any longer than necessary to cook the vegetables through; they should retain their fresh crunch and bright colours. Taste and adjust the seasoning, if needed. To serve, ladle onto warmed plates and sprinkle over the parsley.

**SERVES** 6   **PREP** 20 MINS **COOK** 2 HOURS   **FREEZE** UP TO 3 MONTHS

Cooking lamb on the bone in the pot adds lots more flavour to the dish. If you can't get hold of lamb shanks, neck of lamb would be a good alternative, and will take the same length of time to cook.

# Lamb shanks with harissa and shallots

3–4 tbsp olive oil
2 large lamb shanks
1 tbsp plain flour, seasoned with
   salt and pepper
12 shallots, peeled and left whole
salt and freshly ground black pepper
2 garlic cloves, crushed
125g (4½oz) red lentils, rinsed
   and picked over for stones

400g can chopped tomatoes
600ml (1pint) hot chicken or
   vegetable stock
1 tbsp harissa paste
½ bunch of flat-leaf parsley,
   finely chopped
handful of mint, roughly chopped

**1** Preheat the oven to 150°C (300°F/Gas 2). Heat 1 tbsp of the oil in a large flameproof casserole over a medium-high heat, and toss the lamb shanks in the flour. Cook the shanks in the oil for 5–6 minutes, turning so they become golden on all sides. Top up with oil as needed. Remove and set aside.

**2** Add the remaining oil and reduce the heat to medium. Season the shallots with salt and pepper and cook, stirring, for 8–10 minutes until they begin to colour a little. Stir in the garlic and lentils, then tip in the tomatoes and stock, and bring to the boil. Reduce the heat and stir in the harissa paste, then return the lamb shanks to the casserole.

**3** Cover the casserole with the lid and put in the oven for 2–2½ hours until the lamb is tender and falling off the bone. Check occasionally that it's not drying out, topping up with a little hot water if needed. Shred the meat off the bone and return to the casserole. Add the parsley and mint, and serve with boiled potatoes.

⊙ **SERVES** 4    ◷ **PREP** 20 MINS **COOK** 2¼–2¾ HOURS    ❄ **FREEZE** UP TO 3 MONTHS

Olives, feta cheese, and thyme are all synonymous with Greek cuisine, and here they are combined with a succulent leg of lamb. The feta adds a fabulous saltiness to the finished dish.

# Stuffed lamb, Greek style

1 leg of lamb, boned and butterflied (about 1.8kg/4lb after boning – ask your butcher to do this), or use a boneless shoulder
salt and freshly ground black pepper
2 tbsp olive oil
1 tbsp dried oregano

2 red peppers, deseeded and finely chopped
60g (2oz) stoned black olives, finely chopped
175g (6oz) feta cheese, finely chopped
3 red onions, roughly chopped
4–6 tomatoes, roughly chopped
450ml (15fl oz) red wine
few sprigs of thyme

**1** Preheat the oven to 160°C (325°F/Gas 3). Lay the lamb out flat and season well. Rub both sides all over with the oil and oregano. Cover one side of the lamb with the red peppers, then the olives, and then the feta. Starting from one end, roll up the lamb, tucking in any loose pieces to neaten it. Tie it up with butcher's string so it is secure.

**2** Heat a large flameproof casserole over a medium heat, add the lamb, and cook for 4–6 minutes on each side until it begins to colour. Throw in the red onions and tomatoes and cook for a minute more, then pour in the wine. Bring to the boil, then reduce to a simmer and add some seasoning and the thyme. Cover with the lid and put in the oven for 2–2½ hours or until cooked to your liking. Check occasionally that it's not drying out, topping up with a little hot water if needed.

**3** Remove from the oven, cover the meat loosely with foil, and leave to rest for 15 minutes. Remove the string and carve into slices. Serve with some of the sauce, together with baby roast potatoes with rosemary, and some wilted spinach.

⊘ **SERVES** 4–6    🕐 **PREP** 30 MINS **COOK** 2¼–2¾ HOURS

Instead of the traditional Sunday roast, try this lamb recipe that renders the meat meltingly tender and boasts a delicious coating that mixes with the sauce as it cooks.

# Lamb with parsley, tomato, and breadcrumbs

2kg (4½lb) leg of lamb
1 tbsp olive oil
3 large onions, sliced
handful of rosemary
about 600ml (1 pint) white wine

**For the rub**
bunch of flat-leaf parsley
30g (1oz) sun-dried tomatoes
2 garlic cloves, peeled
85g (3oz) fine breadcrumbs, toasted
2 tbsp olive oil
salt and freshly ground black pepper

**1** Preheat the oven to 160°C (325°F/Gas 3). First make the rub by putting the ingredients into a food processor and pulsing until blended. Set aside.

**2** Wipe the meat, season it well, then stab it all over with a sharp knife. Heat the oil in a large flameproof casserole over a medium-high heat, add the lamb, and fry for about 8 minutes, turning until it is evenly browned. Remove the meat from the casserole and rub the parsley mixture all over it and into all the cuts. Set aside.

**3** Add the onions to the casserole, reduce the heat to medium, and cook for about 10 minutes, until softened. Season with salt and pepper, then sit the lamb on top of the onions, add the rosemary, and pour over the wine. Cover with the lid and put in the oven for 3 hours. Check occasionally that it's not drying out, topping up with a little hot water if needed. Remove from the oven, discard the rosemary, loosely cover the meat with foil, and leave it to rest for about 15 minutes. Serve with minted peas and new potatoes.

⦿ **SERVES** 4–6　🕐 **PREP** 20 MINS **COOK** 3¼ HOURS

Here is a light stew that is best served during the spring when lamb is particularly full of flavour. Broad beans and dill complement each other perfectly – and, of course, the meat.

# Lamb with artichokes, broad beans, and dill

1.25kg (2¾lb) lamb shoulder, with bones, trimmed and cut into bite-sized pieces
salt and freshly ground black pepper
2 tbsp olive oil
2 onions, roughly chopped
3 carrots, peeled and roughly chopped
1 tbsp plain flour
120ml (4fl oz) dry white wine

900ml (1½ pints) hot vegetable stock
few sprigs of rosemary
grated zest of ½ lemon and juice of 1 lemon
675g (1½lb) antipasti artichoke hearts, drained
140g (5oz) frozen or fresh broad beans
bunch of dill, finely chopped

**1** Preheat the oven to 180°C (350°F/Gas 4). Season the meat with salt and pepper. Heat half the oil in a large flameproof casserole over a high heat, add the lamb (in batches, if necessary), and cook for 6–8 minutes until no longer pink. Remove from the casserole and set aside.

**2** Heat the remaining oil in the casserole over a medium heat, add the onions, and cook for 3–4 minutes until soft. Season with salt and pepper, add the carrots, and cook for a further 5 minutes. Sprinkle over the flour, stir, and cook for a couple of minutes. Add the wine, increase the heat, and cook the sauce for a minute.

**3** Pour in the stock and add the rosemary, lemon juice and zest, and lamb. Bring to the boil, reduce to a simmer, cover, and put in the oven for 1 hour. Check occasionally that it's not drying out, topping up with a little hot water if needed. Stir through the artichokes and broad beans and cook for a further 30 minutes. Taste and season as required, and add the dill to taste. Serve with crusty bread.

⊘ **SERVES** 4–6   🕐 **PREP** 15 MINS **COOK** 1¾ HOURS   ❄ **FREEZE** UP TO 1 MONTH

Legend has it that one of Louis XIV's mistresses created this dish in an attempt to stay in the king's good graces. It is delicious, with its succulent chops between layers of sliced potatoes and onions.

# Lamb chops champvallon

1 tbsp olive oil
6–8 lamb loin chops, each 2.5cm (1in)
   thick, (total weight about 1kg/2¼lb),
   trimmed of any excess fat
4 onions, thinly sliced
1.1kg (2½lb) baking potatoes, peeled
   and very thinly sliced
small bunch of thyme, leaves chopped,
   plus a few sprigs, to serve
salt and freshly ground black pepper
3 garlic cloves, finely chopped
about 1 litre/1¾ pints hot
   vegetable stock

**1** Preheat the oven to 180°C (350°F/Gas 4). Heat the oil in a large flameproof casserole over a high heat. Add the chops and cook for 1–2 minutes on each side, until well browned. Remove from the casserole and set aside.

**2** Pour off all but about 1 tbsp of fat from the casserole. Add the onions and cook over a medium heat for 3–4 minutes until soft. Transfer to a large bowl.

**3** Gently stir the potato slices into the softened onions and thyme leaves and season with salt and pepper. Brush a 23 x 32cm (9 x 13in) baking dish with oil. Spread half the potato mixture on the dish, then sprinkle with the garlic. Arrange the chops on top. Cover with the remaining potato, arranging the slices neatly in rows. Pour over enough stock to come just to the top of the potatoes. Bake, uncovered, for 2 hours, or until the lamb and potatoes are tender when pierced. Serve the chops, potatoes, and onion with a spoonful of the cooking liquid, garnished with sprigs of thyme.

**SERVES** 4  **PREP** 25 MINS **COOK** 2¼ HOURS

The meatballs impart all their wonderful flavours in a tomato sauce made smoky with paprika. Use fresh tomatoes if you prefer – roast or griddle them, then liquidize and add to the sauce.

# Lamb meatballs in a tomato sauce

½ onion, roughly chopped
1 chilli, deseeded and roughly chopped
2 garlic cloves, peeled and left whole
100g (3½oz) chorizo, roughly chopped
500g (1lb 2oz) minced lamb
pinch of sweet or hot smoked paprika
salt and freshly ground black pepper
2 tbsp plain flour
4 tbsp olive oil

**For the tomato sauce**
1 onion, finely chopped
3 garlic cloves, finely chopped
120ml (4fl oz) red wine
2 x 400g cans whole tomatoes
1 tsp sweet or hot smoked paprika
1 tbsp chipotle sauce or a splash of
    smoked Tabasco sauce

**1** Preheat the oven to 150°C (300°F/Gas 2). To make the meatballs, put the onion, chilli, and garlic into a food processor and whiz until finely chopped. Add the chorizo and pulse until combined. Tip the mixture into a bowl, stir in the lamb and paprika, and season with salt and pepper. Mix to a paste with your hands. Roll the mixture into small balls and dust each one with a little flour. Heat some of the oil in a large flameproof casserole and cook the meatballs (in batches and with extra oil, if necessary), until brown all over. Remove and set aside. Pour off all but about 2 tbsp of fat from the casserole.

**2** To make the sauce, cook the onion in the casserole over a medium heat for 3–4 minutes until soft. Stir in the garlic and wine, and let the sauce bubble for a minute. Tip in the tomatoes, bring to the boil, then reduce to a simmer. Stir in the smoked paprika and chipotle or Tabasco sauce and add seasoning. Return the meatballs to the casserole and push them so they sit just under the sauce. Cover and put in the oven for 2 hours. Check occasionally that it's not drying out, topping up with a little hot water if needed. Serve the meatballs and sauce piled over spaghetti.

⊚ **SERVES** 4–6    🕐 **PREP** 30 MINS **COOK** 2½ HOURS    ❄ **FREEZE** UP TO 3 MONTHS

There are numerous versions of the "daube", but all are cooked in red wine. Choose a robust wine that you would happily drink. Throw in a cinnamon stick, if you wish, for a touch of warm spice

# Provençal lamb daube with olives

1 orange, zest peeled in wide strips
2 garlic cloves, finely chopped
500ml (16fl oz) red wine
2 bay leaves
3–4 sprigs each of rosemary, thyme, and parsley
10 peppercorns
900g (2lb) boned lamb shoulder, cut into large cubes
2 tbsp olive oil

salt and freshly ground black pepper
300g (10oz) piece of smoked streaky bacon, cut into 5mm (¼in) lardons
400g can chopped tomatoes
2 onions, sliced
2 carrots, peeled and sliced
175g (6oz) mushrooms, trimmed and sliced
140g (5oz) stoned green olives
250ml (9fl oz) hot beef stock

**1** To make the marinade, combine the orange zest, garlic, wine, bay leaves, herbs, and peppercorns in a bowl. Add the lamb and mix well. Pour the oil on top and add seasoning. Cover and refrigerate, turning occasionally, and leave to marinate for 2 hours or up to 12 hours if time permits.

**2** Preheat the oven to 150°C (300°F/Gas 2). Put the bacon in a large heavy-based pan of water, bring to the boil, and blanch for 5 minutes. Drain and rinse with cold water. Remove the lamb from the marinade and dry on kitchen paper. Strain the marinade, reserving the liquid, bay leaf, and zest.

**3** Put the bacon into a casserole and cover with the lamb. Layer the tomatoes and onions on top, then the carrots, mushrooms, and olives. Pour in the strained marinade and stock, season with pepper, and add the bay leaf and zest. Bring to the boil, cover, and put in the oven for 3½–4 hours. Check occasionally that it's not drying out, topping up with hot water if needed. Remove the bay leaf and zest, and season if needed. Serve with mashed potatoes

**SERVES** 4–6    **PREP** 45–50 MINS, PLUS MARINATING    **FREEZE** UP TO 3 MONTHS
**COOK** 3¾–4¼ HOURS

Lamb with sweet squash is the perfect combination and the minced meat benefits from long, slow cooking. Stirring mint and oregano leaves into the dish adds a distinct freshness.

# Lamb mince and squash with green chillies

2 tbsp olive oil
1 butternut squash, peeled, deseeded,
    and chopped into bite-sized pieces
salt and freshly ground black pepper
1 onion, finely chopped
handful of fresh oregano, leaves only,
    or 1 tsp dried oregano
handful of thyme, leaves only
3 garlic cloves, finely chopped

1 green chilli, deseeded and finely chopped
450g (1lb) lamb mince
900ml (1½ pints) hot vegetable stock
400g can chopped tomatoes
60g (2oz) sultanas
bunch of mint leaves, finely chopped
1–2 tsp harissa paste, depending on
    how spicy you like it

**1** Preheat the oven to 180°C (350°F/Gas 4). Heat half the oil in a large flameproof casserole over a medium heat and add the squash. Season with salt and pepper and cook for 5–8 minutes, stirring, until it starts to turn golden. Remove the squash from the casserole and set aside.

**2** Heat the remaining oil in the casserole, add the onion, and cook for 3–4 minutes until soft. Stir through the oregano, thyme, garlic, and chilli and cook for a few more minutes. Add the mince, increase the heat a little, and cook, stirring, for 5–8 minutes until it is no longer pink. Reduce the heat, return the squash to the casserole, add the stock and tomatoes, and bring to the boil. Reduce to a simmer, stir through the sultanas, cover with the lid, and put in the oven for 1–1½ hours. Check occasionally that it's not drying out, topping up with a little hot water if needed.

**3** Taste and season, if necessary, then stir through the mint and harissa paste. Serve with rice or warmed pitta bread and a lightly dressed crisp green salad.

**SERVES** 4–6     **PREP** 25 MINS **COOK** 1½–2 HOURS     **FREEZE** UP TO 1 MONTH

Dried fruit works well with a fatty meat such as pork belly – it creates a delicious, sweet sauce that cuts through the richness. The earthiness of celeriac is a great addition.

# Belly pork and prunes

1 tbsp olive oil
1.1kg (2½lb) pork belly, cut into
  bite-sized pieces
salt and freshly ground black pepper
1 onion, finely sliced
3 garlic cloves, finely chopped
1 tbsp sherry vinegar
120ml (4fl oz) white wine
900ml (1½ pints) hot vegetable stock
  140g (5oz) soft prunes, finely chopped
6 sage leaves, finely shredded
600g (1lb 5oz) celeriac, peeled and
  chopped into bite-sized pieces

**1** Preheat the oven to 160°C (325°F/Gas 3). Heat half the oil in a large flameproof casserole over a high heat and season the pork belly with salt and pepper. Add the pork (in batches, if necessary), skin-side down, and cook until it turns golden and begins to crisp a little. Remove and sit the pork on kitchen paper to drain.

**2** Heat the remaining oil in the casserole over a medium heat, add the onion, and cook for 3–4 minutes until soft. Then stir in the garlic and cook for a minute more. Increase the heat and add the sherry vinegar, letting it simmer for 2–3 minutes. Pour in the wine and continue to boil for a few more minutes until the alcohol evaporates.

**3** Add the stock and stir to scrape up the bits from the bottom of the casserole. Return the pork to the casserole and stir in the prunes, sage, and celeriac. Bring back to the boil, cover, and put in the oven for 2½–3 hours. Check occasionally that it's not drying out, topping up with a little hot water if needed. Taste and season more if needed, and serve with creamy mashed potatoes.

⊘ **SERVES** 4–6    🕐 **PREP** 15 MINS **COOK** 3–3½ HOURS

This combination of rich pork and salty clams – and, indeed, any pork with shellfish – has been enjoyed for centuries in Portugal. A squeeze of lemon at the end brings out the flavours.

# Pork and clam cataplana

900g (2lb) pork tenderloin, cut
   into 2.5cm (1in) cubes
2 tbsp olive oil
1 large onion, thinly sliced
2 garlic cloves, finely chopped
400g can whole tomatoes
1 tbsp tomato purée
dash of Tabasco sauce (or more to taste)
1kg (2¼lb) clams, such as amandes,
   scrubbed (discard any that do
   not close when tapped)
bunch of parsley, leaves chopped

**For the marinade**
2 garlic cloves, finely chopped
1 bay leaf
1½ tbsp paprika
1 tbsp olive oil
375ml (13fl oz) dry white wine
pinch of freshly ground black pepper

**1** To make the marinade, put all the ingredients into a bowl and whisk to combine. Add the pork and mix well. Cover and refrigerate for 2 hours, or 12 hours if time permits, stirring occasionally. Preheat the oven to 180°C (350°F/Gas 4). Lift the meat from the marinade with a slotted spoon and pat dry with kitchen paper. Reserve the marinade. Heat the oil in a large flameproof casserole over a medium-high heat. Add the pork, in batches, and brown well on all sides. Transfer to a bowl and set aside.

**2** Reduce the heat and add the onion and garlic to the casserole. Cover and cook very gently for about 15 minutes, until the onion is very soft and brown. Add the tomatoes, tomato purée, Tabasco, and pork. Pour in the marinade and stir. Cover with the lid and cook in the oven for 1½–1¾ hours, until tender when pierced. Check occasionally that it's not drying out, topping up with a little hot water if needed. Arrange the clams on top of the pork, cover with the lid, and cook in the oven for 15–20 minutes longer until the clams open (discard any that do not open). Transfer to a warmed serving bowl, remove the bay leaf, sprinkle with the parsley, and serve with lemon wedges on the side.

**SERVES** 4   **PREP** 20 MINS, PLUS MARINATING **COOK** 2¼–2½ HOURS   **FREEZE** UP TO 1 MONT.
WITHOUT THE CLAMS

Pear makes the perfect partner to venison and is tasty served with steamed Savoy cabbage with butter and black pepper. You could use beef instead of venison, cooking it for the same length of time.

# Venison stew with pears

2 tsp black peppercorns, crushed
2 tsp juniper berries, crushed
4 shallots, roughly chopped
2 garlic cloves, peeled and left whole
2 onions, quartered
2 carrots, peeled and roughly sliced
1 bouquet garni
2 tbsp red wine vinegar
750ml (1¼ pints) dry red wine

1kg (2¼lb) stewing venison (leg or
   shoulder), fat trimmed and cut
   into 4cm (1½in) cubes
3 tbsp vegetable oil
30g (1oz) plain flour
750ml (1¼ pints) hot beef stock
salt and freshly ground black pepper
4 ripe pears, peeled, cored, and chopped
3 tbsp redcurrant jelly

**1** To make the marinade, put the spices, vegetables, bouquet garni, vinegar, and wine in a pan and bring to the boil, then simmer for about 2 minutes. Transfer to a shallow dish and leave to cool. Add the venison, stir to coat evenly, cover, and refrigerate for 6–8 hours, turning occasionally.

**2** Preheat the oven to 180°C (350°F/Gas 4). Remove the venison and pat dry. Strain the marinade, reserving the bouquet garni, vegetables, and marinade separately. Heat half the oil in a large flameproof casserole over a high heat, add the venison (in batches and with extra oil, if necessary) and cook for 3–5 minutes until brown all over. Transfer to a bowl. Heat the remaining oil over a medium heat, add the reserved vegetables, and cook, stirring, for 5–7 minutes until they start to brown. Add the flour and cook, stirring, for 3–5 minutes until it has been absorbed. Stir in the marinade, venison, bouquet garni, stock, and seasoning. Cover and cook in the oven for 1¼–1½ hours until tender. Stir in the pears and redcurrant jelly and cook for 6–8 minutes until the pears are tender.

**SERVES** 6　**PREP** 30 MINS, PLUS MARINATING **COOK** 1½–1¾ HOURS　**FREEZE** UP TO 3 MONTHS

Slow-cooked sweet cabbage is the perfect complement to ham, and with the addition of spices and dried fruit, the humble piece of meat is transformed. Ham hocks are also known as knuckles.

# Ham hock with red cabbage

2 ham hocks, about 1.35kg (3lb) each
1 red cabbage, cored and finely shredded
2 onions, sliced
4 garlic cloves, finely chopped
few sprigs of thyme
60g (2oz) raisins
pinch of freshly grated nutmeg
pinch of ground cinnamon
300ml (10fl oz) white wine vinegar
600ml (1 pint) hot vegetable stock
salt and freshly ground black pepper

**1** Preheat the oven to 160°C (325°F/Gas 3). Sit the ham hocks in a large heavy-based pan and cover with water. Bring to the boil, then reduce to a simmer, partially cover, and cook gently for 1 hour. Remove the hams and reserve the stock, if you wish to use it instead of the vegetable stock (it can be salty). When the hams are cool enough to handle, remove the skin and discard, then sit the hams in a large flameproof casserole.

**2** Add all the other ingredients to the casserole, using either the stock or the cooking liquid, and tuck the hams in neatly. Season with salt and pepper, cover, and put in the oven for 2 hours. Check occasionally that it's not drying out, topping up with a little hot water if necessary. Remove the hams, shred the meat, and stir it into the casserole. Serve with baked or roast potatoes.

**SERVES** 4–6 **PREP** 20 MINS **COOK** 3 HOURS

Knuckle or ham hock is amazing value, and tasty, too. The Jerusulem artichokes add a nutty, creamy texture, but if they're not available you can use parsnips instead.

# Pot roast smoked ham

2 smoked ham hocks (knuckles),
   about 1.35kg (3lb) each
1 bay leaf
1 tbsp olive oil
1 onion, finely chopped
salt and freshly ground black pepper
3 garlic cloves, finely chopped
few sprigs of thyme
3 carrots, peeled and chopped
225g (8oz) Jerusalem artichokes,
   peeled and sliced
125g (4½oz) yellow split peas
100ml (3½fl oz) dry cider
900ml (1½ pints) hot vegetable stock

**1** Put the ham hocks and bay leaf in a large heavy-based pan, cover with water, and cook for about 2 hours, skimming away any scum that comes to the top of the pan. Remove the ham and, when cool enough to handle, peel away the skins and discard. Set the hams aside. (You can reserve the stock and use it if you wish, but it can be salty.)

**2** Preheat the oven to 180°C (350°F/Gas 4). Heat the oil in a large flameproof casserole over medium heat, add the onion, and cook for 3–4 minutes until soft. Season with salt and pepper, stir through the garlic, thyme, carrots, and artichokes, and cook for a few more minutes. Stir through the split peas to coat. Increase the heat and pour in the cider, let it bubble for a minute, then add the stock and bring to the boil. Reduce to a simmer and return the hams, tucking them down as much as possible.

**3** Cover and put in the oven for about 1 hour or until the split peas are soft. Check ccasionally that it's not drying out too much, topping up with hot water if needed. The ham meat should now slide off the bone, so remove it with a fork and stir into he casserole. Taste and season, necessary, and serve with some crusty bread.

**SERVES** 4–6   **PREP** 25 MINS **COOK** 3¼ HOURS    **FREEZE** UP TO 1 MONTH

A classic Spanish one-pot meal, this is a fabulously warming dish for a bitterly cold night. There are a lot of different meats here, but make sure the chorizo and morcilla you choose are of good quality.

# Cocido

4 tbsp olive oil
4 small onions, quartered
2 garlic cloves, sliced
4 thick slices belly pork,
   about 500g (1lb 2oz) in total
4 chicken thighs,
   about 300g (10oz) in total
250g (9oz) beef braising steak,
   cut into 4 slices
175g (6oz) tocino or smoked
   streaky bacon, cut into 4 pieces
4 small pork spare ribs,
   150g (5½oz) in total

100ml (3½fl oz) white wine
175g (6oz) chorizo, cut into 4 pieces
175g (6oz) morcilla
1 small ham bone
1 bay leaf
salt and freshly ground black pepper
8 small waxy potatoes
4 carrots, peeled and halved lengthways
400g can chickpeas, drained
1 Savoy cabbage or green cabbage
   heart, quartered
3 tbsp chopped flat-leaf parsley,
   to garnish

**1** Heat 1 tbsp of oil in a large saucepan with the onions and garlic, and fry for 10 minutes, stirring occasionally. Heat the remaining oil in a frying pan and fry the pork, chicken, beef, tocino, and spare ribs in batches until lightly browned on all sides, then transfer to the pan with the onions.

**2** Pour the wine into the frying pan, reduce by half, then pour into the saucepan. Add the chorizo, morcilla, ham bone, and bay leaf to the saucepan, season to taste, then pour in enough cold water to cover.

**3** Bring to the boil, reduce the heat, cover, and simmer for around 1 hour 30 minutes. Add the potatoes and carrots, and continue to cook for 30 minutes. Add the chickpeas and cabbage, and cook for 15 minutes more.

**4** To serve, remove the bay leaf and ham bone, and divide the meat and vegetables between warmed plates. Add a few spoonfuls of the hot broth, and sprinkle with parsley.

**SERVES** 6–8  **PREP** 25 MINS **COOK** 2¾ HOURS

When the weather turns cold, you'll find this thick, winter stew is a simple, pleasing dish. The sausages are poached in the stock, giving them a rather pale appearance and soft texture. For a complete one-pot supper, just add frozen peas for the last five minutes, and stir in a good spoonful of wholegrain mustard.

# Swedish sausage casserole

2 tbsp light olive oil
30g (1oz) unsalted butter
1 onion, roughly chopped
1 leek, white part only,
   trimmed and chopped
1½ tbsp plain flour
1 litre (1¾ pints) hot chicken
   or beef stock

500g (1lb 2oz) waxy or semi-waxy
   potatoes, peeled and cut into
   3cm (1in) chunks
250g (9oz) carrots, cut into 1cm (½in) rounds
8 good-quality fresh pork sausages
1 bay leaf
1 bouquet garni
salt and freshly ground black pepper

**1** In a large, flameproof casserole, heat the oil and butter over a medium heat. Add the onion and leek, and cook gently for 5 minutes, until softened. Sprinkle over the flour, and stir it in well. Continue to cook for a couple of minutes, to brown the flour slightly.

**2** Gradually stir in the stock, and bring to the boil. It should thicken slightly as it heats. When it boils, add the potatoes and carrots.

**3** Prick the sausages with a fork, and add them to the casserole, making sure that everything is submerged.

**4** Add the bay leaf and bouquet garni, and season well. Cover and cook over a low heat for 20–30 minutes, until the vegetables are soft, and the sausages cooked through. The cooking time will depend on the type of potatoes. It is ready once the potatoes are cooked, but be sure not to let them fall apart. Remove the bay leaf and bouquet garni, and serve.

**SERVES** 4   **PREP** 10 MINS **COOK** 35-45 MINS

A simpler version of a classic dish from the Alsace region of France, this one-pot meal is excellent for hearty appetites on a cold night. You can prepare the recipe up to step three, cool, and refrigerate. Fry the sausages and reheat the dish the next day for a speedy supper.

# Choucrôute garnie

3 tbsp goose fat, or sunflower oil
250g (9oz) piece smoked gammon, chopped
500g (1lb 2oz) pork spare ribs, sliced
   to separate
2 onions, chopped
2 green apples, cored and sliced
1 garlic clove, finely chopped
6 black peppercorns, lightly crushed
6 juniper berries, lightly crushed
large sprig of thyme

2 bay leaves
600g jar sauerkraut, thoroughly
   drained and rinsed
300ml (10fl oz) light beer or
   Riesling wine
500ml (16fl oz) chicken stock
12 small new potatoes
350g (12oz) saucisse de Strasbourg
salt and freshly ground black pepper
chopped flat-leaf parsley, to serve

**1** Heat 2 tablespoons of goose fat in a large, flameproof casserole and fry the gammon and ribs, turning, for 3–4 minutes, or until evenly coloured. Remove the meat and keep warm. Add the onions to the pan and fry for 2–3 minutes.

**2** Add the apples, garlic, peppercorns, juniper berries, thyme, and bay leaves. Stir in the sauerkraut, return the gammon and pork, and pour in the beer (or wine) and stock. Place a piece of greaseproof paper on top, cover tightly with a lid, and simmer over a very low heat for 2 hours.

**3** Add the potatoes, pushing them down into the sauerkraut. Cover and cook on a low heat for 50–60 minutes, or until tender.

**4** Meanwhile, heat the remaining fat in a frying pan, and fry the sausages until brown, turning once. Spoon the sauerkraut mixture on to a large platter and arrange the sausages on top. Season to taste, sprinkle with parsley, and serve.

SERVES 6-8   PREP 30 MINS **COOK** 3 HOURS

This recipe works best with a variety of German-style cooked or scalded sausages. It is conservatively spiced, but feel free to increase the amount of cayenne pepper and smoked paprika for a more vibrant flavour. If you prefer, use your favourite white beans or chickpeas, instead of butterbeans.

# Sausage and butterbean goulash

2 tbsp olive oil
1 onion, finely chopped
1 red pepper, deseeded,
   and cut into 2cm (¾in) dice
1 yellow pepper, deseeded,
   and cut into 2cm (¾in) dice
2 garlic cloves, crushed
1 tbsp plain flour
½ tsp cayenne pepper
½ tsp smoked paprika
400ml (14fl oz) passata

300ml (10fl oz) chicken stock
salt and freshly ground black pepper
400g (14oz) mixed wurst, such as
   Krakauer, Bockwurst, and Lyoner
   Fleischwurst, skinned if necessary
   and cut into 2cm (¾in) chunks
400g can butterbeans, drained
   and rinsed
2 tbsp finely chopped
   flat-leaf parsley
2 tbsp soured cream

**1** In a large, heavy saucepan, heat the oil over a low heat and gently fry the onion and peppers for 5 minutes until softened, but not browned. Add the garlic and cook for a further 2 minutes.

**2** Stir in the flour, cayenne pepper, and smoked paprika, and stir well. Add the passata and chicken stock to the pan, and mix thoroughly. Season with salt and pepper if needed (the stock may be salty). Bring to the boil, reduce the heat, and simmer for 10 minutes.

**3** Add the wurst and continue to simmer for 10 minutes. Add the butterbeans and gently simmer for a final 5 minutes.

**4** Stir in the parsley and serve with the soured cream swirled on top, or on the side, with white rice or crusty bread.

**SERVES** 4    **PREP** 10 MINS **COOK** 35 MINS

A robust dish that will hit the spot on cold days and fill you up. The lentils become soft and tender and, because they are cooked for so long, they are flavoured by the sausages.

# Lentil and Toulouse sausage casserole

2 tbsp olive oil
8 Toulouse sausages, roughly chopped
1 onion, finely chopped
2 carrots, peeled and finely diced
freshly ground black pepper
3 garlic cloves, finely chopped
140g (5oz) chorizo, diced
3 sprigs of rosemary

few sprigs of thyme
200g (7oz) Puy lentils or brown lentils, rinsed and picked over for any stones
175ml (6fl oz) red wine
900ml (1½ pints) hot chicken stock
1 red chilli, left whole
splash of extra virgin olive oil, to serve

**1** Preheat the oven to 160°C (325°F/Gas 3). Heat half the oil in a large flameproof casserole over a high heat, add the Toulouse sausages, and cook for a few minutes until they begin to turn golden. Remove from the casserole and set aside.

**2** Add the remaining oil, stir in the onion and carrot, and turn to coat. Season with pepper and leave to cook for a few minutes, stirring occasionally. Add the garlic, chorizo, and herbs, give it all a stir, then return the Toulouse sausages to the casserole and stir in the lentils. Add the wine, bring to the boil, and cook for a minute.

**3** Pour in the stock, bring to the boil, then reduce to a simmer. Add the chilli, cover with the lid, and put in the oven for 1½ hours. Check occasionally that it's not drying out, topping up with a little hot water if needed. Taste and season, if necessary, remove the whole chilli, then ladle into warmed bowls and serve with a splash of extra virgin olive oil and some crusty bread.

⊘ **SERVES** 4–6   🕐 **PREP** 15 MINS **COOK** 1¾ HOURS   ❄ **FREEZE** UP TO 1 MONTH

Make sure you buy a smoky Cajun-style andouille sausage for this hearty dish from the American South, rather than the French andouille, which is made mostly from the intestines and stomach of the pig. Leave the seeds in the chilli for a spicy kick, or omit them for a milder result.

# Cajun andouille gumbo

2 tbsp olive oil
1 large onion, finely chopped
1 green pepper, deseeded
   and cut into 2cm (¾in) dice
2 garlic cloves, crushed
25g (scant 1oz) unsalted butter
3 tbsp plain flour
2 x 400g cans chopped tomatoes
500ml (16fl oz) fish or chicken stock
2 dried red chillies, finely chopped
1 tsp smoked paprika

200g (7oz) okra, cleaned, trimmed,
   and cut into 2cm (¾in) chunks
250g (9oz) American andouille
   smoked sausage, peeled and
   cut into 2cm (¾in) chunks
salt and freshly ground black pepper
1 tbsp thyme leaves
500g (1lb 2oz) raw king prawns,
   shelled and deveined
2 tbsp finely chopped flat-leaf parsley

**1** Heat the oil in a large, heavy saucepan. Add the onion and green pepper, and fry gently for 5 minutes until soft, but not brown. Add the garlic, and continue to cook for a further 2 minutes.

**2** Add the butter to the pan and allow it to melt, then add the flour and stir on a very low heat for around 10 minutes, until browned. Add the tomatoes, stock, chillies, paprika, okra, and sausage, and bring to the boil. Taste and season with pepper, and salt if necessary (the stock may be salty).

**3** Reduce the heat to a low simmer and add the thyme. Cook, covered, for 30 minutes, stirring occasionally, until the okra is soft and the gumbo well thickened.

**4** Increase the heat and add the prawns. Continue to cook the gumbo, uncovered, for a further 5 minutes, until the prawns are opaque and cooked through. Stir through the parsley, and serve with rice.

**SERVES** 6    **PREP** 15 MINS **COOK** 1 HOUR

# pies and pasties

# Shortcrust pastry

A good shortcrust pastry is light, crisp, and suits all types of pies and tarts. Use the following quantities: 150g (5½oz) plain flour, 75g (2½oz) unsalted butter, or follow the quantities in the recipe you are using.

**1** Rub the plain flour and the unsalted butter, chilled and diced, together with your fingertips until the mix resembles fine breadcrumbs. Work swiftly, handling the pastry as little as possible to avoid the gluten in the flour heating up. Try working in a cool room. To make a richer pastry, add 1 lightly beaten egg yolk at this stage.

**2** Add 3–4 tablespoons cold water and a pinch of salt to the crumbs and bring together to form a soft dough (if you are making a rich shortcrust and have added in an egg yolk at step 1, add just enough water to the crumbs, 1 tbsp at a time, to form a soft dough). Handle the pastry gently and be careful not to overwork it; just work it until the texture is smooth. Add extra water if it is too dry. Wrap in cling film and chill for 30 minutes. You could substitute the butter for lard or use half lard and half butter for some traditional recipes.

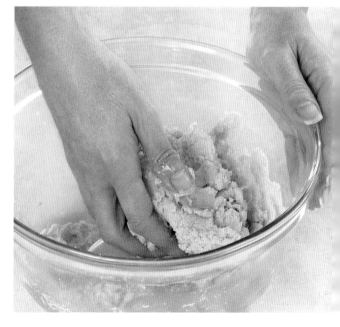

# Sweet shortcrust pastry

The classic shortcrust pastry (see opposite) can be turned into something sweeter. Just substitute 30g (1oz) of the flour for caster sugar, or follow the quantities in the recipe you are using.

**1** Rub the plain flour and the chilled and diced unsalted butter together with your fingertips until the mixture resembles fine breadcrumbs. Work swiftly, handling the pastry as little as possible to avoid the gluten in the flour heating up. Try working in a cool room. Stir in the caster sugar. To make a richer pastry, add 1 lightly beaten egg yolk to the flour mixture.

**2** Add 3–4 tablespoons cold water and bring together to form a soft dough (if you are making a rich shortcrust and have added in an egg yolk at step 1, add just enough water to the crumbs, 1 tbsp at a time, to form a soft dough). Handle the pastry gently and be careful not to overwork it; just work it until the texture is smooth. Add extra water if it is too dry. Wrap in cling film and chill for 30 minutes. If you need to scale up pastry quantities, add extra water instead of more egg.

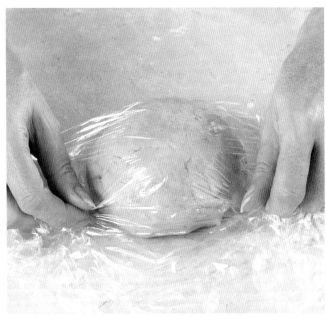

# Wheat-free shortcrust pastry

Ideal for people with a gluten intolerance. Use 225g (8oz) gluten-free plain flour, 1 tsp xanthan gum, a pinch of salt, 100g (3½oz) butter, 1 egg, or follow the quantities in the recipe you are using.

**1** Sift the flour, xanthan gum, and a pinch of salt into a large bowl and mix together to combine. For sweet pastry, add 2 tbsp icing sugar with the flour.

**2** Add the chilled, diced butter and rub it in with your fingertips until the mixture resembles breadcrumbs. Alternatively, pulse in a food processor.

**3** Beat the egg, then add to the mixture and stir it in with a palette knife or a round-bladed table knife until the mixture clumps together.

**4** Add 1–2 tbsp cold water, gradually, a few drops at a time, mixing after each addition. Repeat until it comes together to form a dough.

**5** On a floured surface, knead the dough lightly until smooth. Shape the dough into a ball, then wrap in cling film.

**6** Chill the dough in the refrigerator for 10 minutes until firm. This will make rolling out the pastry easier. Use the pastry as required.

# Suet crust pastry

For this classic pastry, great for a steak and kidney pie, use these quantities: 300g (10oz) self-raising flour, ½ tsp salt, 150g (5½oz) suet, or follow the quantities in the recipe you are using.

**1** Sift the self-raising flour into a large bowl and add the salt. Combine these ingredients by mixing briefly with a wooden spoon.

**2** Dice the beef or vegetable suet into small 1cm (½in) cubes, then add the diced suet to the flour in the bowl and stir in slightly.

**3** Rub the diced suet into the flour with your fingertips until the mixture resembles rough breadcrumbs. Work swiftly, handling the pastry as little as possible to avoid the gluten in the flour heating up. Try working in a cool room.

**4** Add 4–6 tbsp cold water and mix to start to bring the mixture together, first with a wooden spoon, and then using your hands.

**5** Use your fingertips to bring the mixture together to form a soft dough. Handle the pastry gently and be careful not to overwork it; just work it until the texture is smooth. Add more water if the dough is too dry.

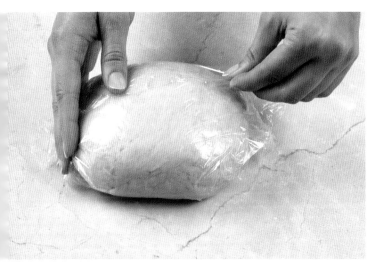

**6** Wrap the pastry in cling film and chill in the refrigerator for at least 30 minutes before using.

# Hot-water crust pastry

This pastry is best for pork pies. Use 400g (14oz) plain flour, ½ tsp fine salt, 150ml (5fl oz) boiling water, 150g (5½oz) cubed lard, or follow the quantities in the recipe you are using.

**1** Sift the flour into a large bowl and add the salt. Using a wooden spoon, mix, and then make a well in the middle of the flour mixture.

**2** Measure the boiling water into a jug and add the diced lard. Stir the mixture with a metal spoon until the fat has melted.

**3** Carefully pour the hot melted fat mixture into the well in the centre of the flour

**4** Stir the mixture with a wooden spoon, starting in the well, to combine all the ingredients, until it starts to come together.

**5** Knead the mixture with your hands into a soft dough, being careful because it will be hot. This pastry must be used quickly, as it begins to harden as it cools. Any pastry kept for tops or lids should be wrapped in a clean tea towel and kept in a warm place until needed.

# Puff pastry

To make this flaky pastry, which is suitable for a variety of sweet and savoury pies, use 250g (9oz) plain flour, ½ tsp salt, 175g (6oz) butter, or follow the quantities in the recipe you are using.

**1** Sift the plain flour and salt into a bowl. Rub in 60g (2oz) diced butter with your fingertips until it resembles breadcrumbs.

**2** Add 100ml (3½fl oz) water and bring it together to form a soft, elastic dough. Wrap in cling film and chill in the refrigerator for 15 minutes.

**3** Turn the dough out onto a lightly floured surface and roll out until it is a large rectangular shape, about 3mm (⅛in) in thickness.

**4** Dot 115g (4oz) diced butter over the top two-thirds of the dough, then fold the unbuttered side over half the buttered side.

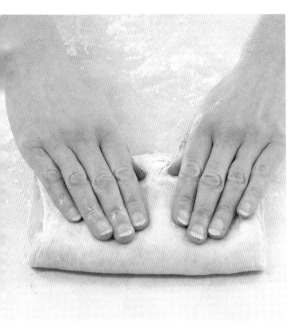

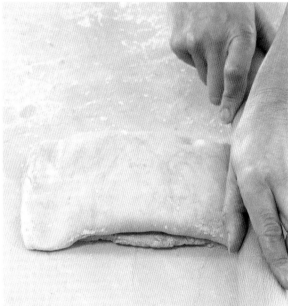

5 Fold the dough over again so the butter is completely enclosed in the layers of dough, then turn the dough over.

6 Roll over the edges of the dough with the rolling pin to seal. Wrap in cling film and chill in the refrigerator for 15 minutes.

7 Lightly re-flour the surface. Repeat the rolling and folding process of step 4, but without adding the butter. Seal, wrap, and chill for 15 minutes.

8 Repeat step 7 three more times, chilling the dough for 15 minutes between each turn. The dough is now ready to use as required.

# Quick puff pastry

This pastry is much quicker to make than the classic puff pastry. Use 250g (9oz) semi-frozen butter, 250g (9oz) plain flour, 1 tsp salt, or follow the quantities in the recipe you are using.

**1** Freeze the butter for 30 minutes. Coarsely grate it into a bowl. Sift over the flour and the salt and rub together until well-combined and crumbly.

**2** Pour in 90–100ml (3–3½fl oz) water. Use a fork to start mixing, then use your fingertips to form a rough dough. If it is too dry, add more water.

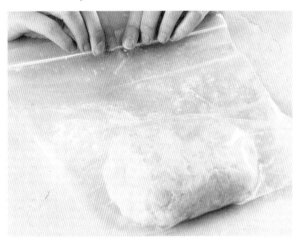

**3** Shape the dough into a ball, then place in a clean plastic bag. Seal the bag and set aside to chill in the refrigerator for 20 minutes.

**4** Thinly roll out the dough on a lightly floured surface to a long rectangle, short sides, about 25cm (10in). Keep the edges straight and even.

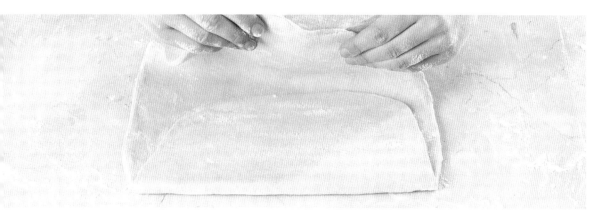

**5** Take one-third of the pastry and fold it into the middle of the rectangle, then fold the remaining third over to make 3 layers. The rolling and folding process incorporates air into the pastry, making it puff up on baking.

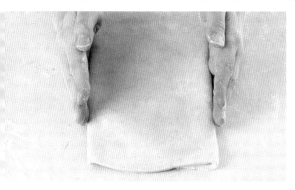

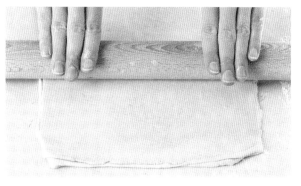

**6** Turn the dough over so the joins are easily sealed when it is re-rolled. Give it a quarter turn so that the folded edges are at the sides.

**7** Roll out the dough again to a similar size as the original rectangle. Make sure to keep the short sides even in size.

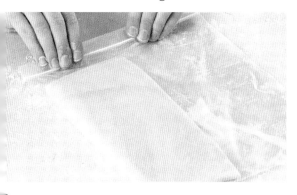

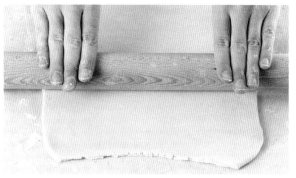

**8** Repeat the folding, turning, and rolling. Put the dough back in the plastic bag and chill in the refrigerator for 20 minutes.

**9** Roll, fold, and turn the pastry twice more, then chill in the refrigerator for a final 20 minutes. The dough is now ready to use as required.

# Strudel pastry

To make a light, delicate strudel pastry, use: 250g (9oz) plain flour, 1 egg, ½ tsp lemon juice and a pinch of salt, or follow the quantities in the recipe you are using.

**1** Sift the plain flour into a mound onto a clean work surface. Then, using your fingers, make a well in the centre of the flour.

**2** Beat the egg with 125ml (4fl oz) water, lemon juice, and a pinch of salt together in a large bowl, then pour the mixture into the well.

**3** Work the ingredients in the well with your fingertips, gradually drawing in the flour to combine into a dough.

**4** Knead just enough flour into the other ingredients so that the dough forms a ball; it should be quite soft.

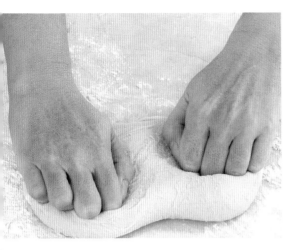

**5** On a floured surface, knead the dough for about 10 minutes until it is shiny, smooth and elastic, then shape the dough into a ball.

**6** On the floured surface, cover the ball of dough with another large clean bowl, and set aside to rest for 30 minutes.

**7** Flour your hands and stretch the dough, starting at the centre and working outwards. Continue to work outwards until the dough is as thin as possible; it should be translucent. The dough is now ready to use as required.

# Cobbler dough

Use these quantities: 225g (8oz) self-raising flour, 2 tbsp baking powder, 75g (2½oz) caster sugar, a pinch of salt, 75g (2½oz) butter, 100ml (3½fl oz) buttermilk, 1 egg, or follow the recipe you are using.

**1** For a cobbler topping, sift the flour, baking powder, caster sugar (omit for a savoury cobbler), and a pinch of salt into a large bowl.

**2** Add the chilled and diced unsalted butter and mix with your fingertips until the mixture resembles breadcrumbs.

**3** Beat together the buttermilk and egg, then add to the dry ingredients, and mix to form a dough.

**4** Put the filling into a baking dish. Place walnut-sized spoonfuls of the dough over the filling; leave space for the mix to spread.

**5** Lightly press down on the balls of mixture to help them combine with the filling and bake. If liked, add chopped herbs or spices to the basic mix to complement the filling.

# Lining a tart tin

Follow these steps to lining any tart tin perfectly every time. Use the tart tin as a template before lining it with the pastry, and take care not to overstretch it or it may shrink when baked.

**1** Roll out the pastry on a lightly floured surface to a large circle, about 3mm (⅛in) thick. Don't use too much flour as it may make the pastry dry.

**2** Roll the pastry up carefully using the rolling pin, then unroll it over the tart tin, making sure it overlaps on all sides.

**3** Push the pastry in with your fingers, gently pressing it into the base and sides of the tin. It should overlap the sides by at least 2cm (¾in).

# Baking blind

To achieve a crisp pastry case, bake the unfilled pastry shell either partially or completely before adding the filling, depending on the recipe. Use dried pulses as an alternative to baking beans.

**1** Prick the bottom of the pastry all over with a fork to stop it puffing up, and line with a piece of baking parchment or greaseproof paper.

**2** Weigh the baking parchment down with baking beans. Place the pastry case on a baking tray – this supports the sides of the pastry until cooked.

**3** Bake blind in the centre of a preheated oven for 20–25 minutes until the sides of the pastry are cooked. Remove the beans and paper.

**4** Return the case to the oven and bake for 5 more minutes to crisp the bottom. Set aside to cool, trimming the edges with a knife while warm.

# Decorative edges

There's nothing like a home-made pie or tart. For an individual finishing touch, don't just stop at neatly trimming the edges, try one of these ideas to make your pastry treats look as special as they taste.

### crimped
Pinch the pastry edge with the forefinger and thumb of your right hand, and make even indentations in the top edge with the forefinger of your left hand.

### fork-crimped
A quick and simple finishing touch that also helps to seal the pastry lid – especially useful if the filling is quite wet. Press down all around the edges of the pie using the tines of a fork.

**feathered**
Using kitchen scissors, snip 2cm (1in) cuts, 1cm (½in) apart, into the edge of the pastry. With your fingertips, fold every alternate flap of pastry back, diagonally, along the edge of the tart. Leave the next flap laying on the edge of the dish. This creates an elegant, feathered effect.

**p**
C
p
to
O
p
M
w
th
o
i

**scalloped**
Press the pastry rim firmly with the forefinger of your left hand and, using the tip of a table knife, indent the pastry either side of your finger.

# Decorative tops

The top of a covered pie can be decorated in a variety of ways with leftover pastry trimmings. You could also make a feature of the steam-hole in a pie – it looks great and stops the pastry going soggy.

**decorative shapes**
Roll out any leftover pastry and design your own shapes, such as leaves, and cut them out using a sharp knife. Or use a small cutter in the shape of a heart, flower, star, numbers, or letters to personalize the pie.

**twisted ribbon**
Cut a 2cm (1in) wide pastry strip, long enough to go around the pie. Hold the strip at one end and twist it from the other end. Moisten the edge of the pie with water and secure the pastry strip in place. Seal the edges together.

## cut-outs

Cut several holes in the centre of the pie lid, using a small cutter in the shape of your choice, such as a leaf, before positioning it on the pie. You could also cut a cross in the lid, when it's in position, and pull back the point of each triangle to create a decorative steam-hole.

## pastry rose

Cut out 4 x 7.5cm (3in) pastry squares and stack them up. Place the squares on one forefinger and pull the corners down to form a ball. Cut a cross half-way through the ball, and open out the layers to create petals.

## lattice top

Roll out any leftover pastry and using a fluted pastry wheel, cut it into 1.5cm (½in) wide strips, long enough to go across the tart. Moisten the tart edges with water and arrange the strips across the filling. Trim to fit all around the outer edge.

Use either home-made or shop-bought shortcrust pastry to make this double-crusted pie. Suitable for vegetarians, its rich, cheesy filling is offset by the sharpness of the onions.

# Cheese and onion pie

**For the filling**
1 tbsp olive oil
1 large onion, finely chopped
salt and freshly ground black pepper
2 eggs
200g (7oz) mature Cheddar cheese, grated

**For the pastry**
350g (12oz) ready-made shortcrust pastry
   (or to make your own, see p228)
plain flour, for dusting

**1** Preheat the oven to 200°C (400°F/Gas 6). Heat the olive oil in a small pan over a low heat. Add the onion and a pinch of salt, and sweat for 2 minutes until transparent and just starting to soften. Tip into a bowl and set aside to cool completely.

**2** Lightly beat 1 of the eggs in a small bowl and stir into the cooled onion with the cheese. Season with salt and black pepper.

**3** Halve the pastry, then roll out each piece on a floured surface. Use one of the pastry circles to line a 18cm (7in) round pie tin, allowing the pastry to hang over the edge, and fill with the cheese and onion mixture. Dampen the edge of the pastry with water, then top with the other circle of pastry. Trim away the excess pastry. Using your thumb and finger, pinch the edges of the pastry together to seal. Cut 2 slits in the top to allow the steam to escape.

**4** Lightly beat the remaining egg and brush all over the top of the pie. Bake for 25–35 minutes until cooked and golden. Serve with a mixed salad and boiled or steamed new potatoes.

**SERVES** 4   **PREP** 15 MINS PLUS COOLING **COOK** 40 MINS   **FREEZE** UP TO 6 MONTHS

These delicious individual slices make a light, tasty vegetarian alternative to pork pies. Good served warm or cold, they transport well and make a perfect picnic pie or lunchbox treat.

# Mediterranean jalousie

**For the pastry**
500g (1lb 2oz) ready-made puff pastry
  (or to make your own, see pp236–9)
plain flour, for dusting
beaten egg or milk, to glaze

**For the filling**
3 tbsp green pesto
200g (7oz) mozzarella cheese,
  cut into 1cm (½in) cubes, or grated
140g (5oz) artichokes in oil, drained
140g (5oz) sun-dried tomatoes
  in oil, drained
30g (1oz) pitted green olives
freshly ground black pepper

**1** Preheat the oven to 220°C (425°F/Gas 7). Roll out just less than half the pastry on a lightly floured surface to a 30 x 15cm (12 x 6in) rectangle, then place the pastry on a large dampened baking tray. Roll out the remaining pastry to a 30 x 18cm (12 x 7in) rectangle, lightly dust with flour, then fold in half lengthways. Make cuts 1cm (½in) apart along the folded edge to within 2.5cm (1in) of the outer edge.

**2** Spread the pesto over the pastry on the baking tray to within 2.5cm (1in) of the edges, and top with half the cheese. Pat the artichokes and tomatoes with kitchen paper to remove any excess oil, and arrange on top of the cheese with the olives. Scatter with the remaining cheese and season to taste with black pepper.

**3** Dampen the edges of the pastry with water. Carefully place the second piece of pastry on top and press the edges together to seal; trim away the excess. Brush the top with beaten egg and bake for 25 minutes, or until golden brown and crisp. Set aside to cool for a few minutes before slicing and serving. This is good served with a green salad.

**SERVES** 4    **PREP** 20 MINS **COOK** 25 MINS

Make sure you chill these pasties in the refrigerator before baking. This helps firm up the pastry and hold them together while cooking. These much-loved, wholesome pies are delicious hot or cold.

# Spinach and potato pasties

**For the pastry**
150g (5½oz) plain wholemeal flour
150g (5½oz) plain flour,
    plus extra for dusting
150g (5½oz) butter, cold and cubed
½tsp salt
1 egg, beaten, to glaze

**For the filling**
300g (10oz) unpeeled waxy potatoes, such
    as charlotte, cut into small chunks
225g (8oz) spinach
1 garlic clove, finely chopped
250g (9oz) ricotta cheese
75g (2½oz) Grana Padano cheese, grated
freshly grated nutmeg
salt and freshly ground black pepper

**1** To make the pastry, rub both flours and butter together with your fingertips until the mixture resembles breadcrumbs. Add the salt and about 4 tbsp cold water, to bring the mixture together to form a soft dough. Wrap and chill for 30 minutes.

**2** For the filling, cook the potato in a saucepan of boiling water for 10 minutes. Drain and set aside to cool. Place the spinach in a colander and pour boiling water over it to wilt. Squeeze out all the liquid and chop finely. Place the spinach in a large bowl with the garlic, cheeses, nutmeg, salt, and black pepper, and stir well. Set aside.

**3** Preheat the oven to 190°C (375°F/Gas 5). Line two baking trays with baking parchment. Stir the cooled potato into the spinach and cheese mixture.

**4** Cut dough into 4 equal pieces. On a floured surface, roll each piece into a circle about 20cm (8in) across and 5mm (¼in) thick. Using a small plate (about 20cm/8in in diameter) cut a circle from each round of dough. Arrange a quarter of the filling on half of each pastry circle, leaving a 1cm (½in) border around the edge. Brush edges with the beaten egg, bring them together to seal, and crimp for a decorative finish. Chill for 10 minutes.

**5** Place pasties on the prepared baking trays and brush with the remaining beaten egg. Cut a slit in the top of each pasty and bake for 20–25 minutes. Serve hot or cold.

**SERVES** 4     **PREP** 45 MINS PLUS CHILLING **COOK** 30-35 MINS     **FREEZE** UP TO 1 MONTH

Spinach seems to work well with strong, sharp cheeses, such as Stilton, goat's cheese, or feta. Here, the classic filling is given a makeover, encased in a filo pie with herbs, and baked until crisp.

# Herby feta filo pie

**For the filling**
900g (2lb) spinach, rinsed
100g (3½oz) butter,
    plus extra for greasing
2 onions and garlic cloves, finely chopped
120g (4oz) roasted peppers in oil,
    drained and chopped
a handful of basil leaves

3 tbsp mint leaves, chopped
3 tbsp parsley, chopped
salt and freshly ground black pepper
300g (10oz) feta cheese, crumbled

**For the pastry**
6 sheets ready-made filo pastry,
    40 x 30cm (16 x 12in)

**1** Pack the spinach leaves into a large saucepan, cover, and cook for 8–10 minutes until just wilted. Drain well. Set aside, still draining, to cool.

**2** Melt 25g (scant 1oz) butter until bubbling and gently fry the onions, stirring occasionally, for 3 minutes. Add the garlic and fry for a further 2 minutes. Stir in the peppers and herbs, and set aside. Preheat the oven to 200°C (400°F/Gas 6). Grease and line a 20cm (8in) round springform baking tin.

**3** Blot the spinach with kitchen paper, then chop finely. Stir into the onion mixture, and season to taste. Melt the remaining butter. Brush the prepared tin with a little melted butter and line with a sheet of pastry, leaving the edges to overhang. Brush pastry with more melted butter. Repeat, layering the 5 remaining sheets of pastry, brushing the surface of each with melted butter and leaving the edges overhanging. Add half the filling, then the feta cheese, then the remaining filling. Fold the overhanging pastry over the filling to cover.

**4** Brush the top of the pastry with any remaining butter and place the tin on a baking tray. Bake for 35–40 minutes until crisp and golden. Be sure to leave the pie to stand for 10 minutes before carefully releasing from the tin. Serve hot or warm, cut into wedges. Good with a crisp salad or seasonal vegetables.

If you don't have much time, use shop-bought puff pastry, rather than making your own. Buy a butter-based one, and it will be all but indistinguishable from the home-made variety.

# Sweet potato, red onion, and thyme galettes with chilli

**For the filling**
2 medium-sized sweet potatoes, 300g (10oz) peeled weight
2 red onions, cut into 1cm (½in) cubes
1 tbsp olive oil
salt and freshly ground black pepper
½ red chilli, deseeded and finely chopped
1 tsp finely thyme, chopped

**For the pastry**
375g (12oz) ready-made puff pastry
   (or to make your own, see pp236–9)
plain flour, for dusting
1 egg yolk, beaten

**1** Preheat the oven to 200°C (400°F/Gas 6). Dice the sweet potatoes into 1cm (½in) cubes. Toss the sweet potato and red onions in the olive oil in a large bowl and season well with salt and black pepper. Turn the vegetables out onto a baking tray and bake for 30 minutes until softened and golden at the edges.

**2** Roll out the puff pastry on a lightly floured surface into a square about 30 x 40cm (12 x 16in) and cut it into quarters. Lay the pastry rectangles on one or two baking trays, and brush them with beaten egg yolk.

**3** Toss the cooked vegetables with the chopped chilli and thyme, and divide the mixture equally between the four pastry rectangles. Spread the vegetables out, leaving a 1cm (½in) clear edge to the pastry.

**4** Bake the galettes for 20 minutes, or until the pastry is puffed up and golden brown at the edges, and the bottom is firm to the touch and golden. Set aside to cool for 5 minutes before serving with a leafy green salad. Cooked galettes can be stored in the refrigerator for up to 2 days and warmed through again before serving.

**SERVES** 4    **PREP** 20 MINS **COOK** 50 MINS

A fabulous dinner-party dish, this is more of a deconstructed pie. The layers of buttery puff pastry are made crisp and flat by sandwiching them in between two baking trays halfway through cooking.

# Halibut and spinach pies

**For the pastry**
300g (10oz) sheet puff pastry
  (or to make your own, see pp236–9)
plain flour, for dusting
1 tbsp butter, for brushing

**For the filling**
4 x 125g (4½oz) halibut fillets,
salt and freshly ground black pepper

a large knob of unsalted butter
2 tbsp olive oil
1 garlic clove, crushed
200g (7oz) ready-washed
baby spinach leaves
8 tbsp ready-made hollandaise sauce
grated zest of ½ lemon

**1** Preheat the oven to 190°C (375°F/Gas 5). Roll out pastry on a floured surface to 5mm (¼in) thick. Cut the pastry into 8 equal rectangles, about 12 x 7cm (5 x 2¾in). They should be the same size as the fish. Score a diagonal stripe across the rectangles, taking care not to cut right through the pastry. Melt the butter and use to brush the pastry pieces well.

**2** Use a fish slice to place the pastry pieces on a baking tray. Bake for 5–7 minutes until they start to colour and puff up. Place a similarly sized baking tray on top of the pastry, pushing down firmly, then bake for another 7–10 minutes until the pastry is flat, crisp, and golden.

**3** Season the fish fillets well on both sides. Fry in 1 tbsp butter and 1 tbsp olive oil for 2–3 minutes each side, until they are just firm to the touch when gently pressed in the centre.

**4** Heat the remaining butter and olive oil in a large pan. Add the garlic and cook for 1–2 minutes, until soft. Add the spinach, season well, and cook for 2–3 minutes, stirring, until just wilted. Heat hollandaise sauce in a small pan over a gentle heat until warmed through. Add lemon zest and season with black pepper.

**5** Place a piece of pastry on each serving plate. Cover with spinach, then spread 1 tbsp warm hollandaise over the spinach and place a fish fillet on top. Cover with another spoonful of hollandaise and top with the remaining pastry. Serve.

 **SERVES** 4  **PREP** 10 MINS **COOK** 25 MINS

Here a traditional mashed potato-topped fish pie is given a grown-up twist with the use of succulent king prawns. The mustard should complement the filling, not overwhelm it, so taste as you go.

# Salmon and prawn pie

**For the topping**
900g (2lb) potatoes, peeled and quartered
salt and freshly ground black pepper
2 tbsp milk

**For the filling**
350g (12oz) cooked salmon,
flaked into chunks
350g (12oz) hot-smoked salmon fillets,
flaked into chunks

200g (7oz) prawns, cooked,
peeled, and deveined
salt and freshly ground black pepper
30g (1oz) butter
30g (1oz) plain flour
450ml (15fl oz) milk
2 tbsp chives, chopped
1 tbsp capers in brine,
rinsed and drained
60g (2oz) Cheddar cheese, grated
30g (1oz) fresh white breadcrumbs

**1** Preheat the oven to 200°C (400°F/Gas 6). Cook the potatoes in a large saucepan of boiling salted water for 15 minutes, or until soft. Drain the potatoes, return to the pan and mash well until there are no lumps. Add the 2 tbsps milk, mash again until smooth, then season to taste with salt and black pepper. Set aside.

**2** Arrange the smoked salmon, and prawns in a 20 x 30cm (8 x 12in) ovenproof dish so that they are evenly distributed. Season with salt and black pepper, and set aside.

**3** Gently melt the butter in a pan over a low heat. Remove from the heat and stir in the flour with a wooden spoon. Add a little milk and beat until smooth. Return the pan to the heat, and continue adding the milk, a little at a time, stirring constantly, until the sauce has thickened. Whisk to get rid of any lumps, then stir in the chives and capers.

**4** Pour the sauce over the prawns and salmon, and stir well. Cover with the mashed potato. Combine the cheese and breadcrumbs, season well, and sprinkle evenly over the mash. Bake for 15–20 minutes until heated through and the topping is crisp and golden.

Haddock is the fish of choice in this traditional family dish, but you can use your favourite white fish if you like. Serve the pie with steamed broccoli or fresh peas for a healthy midweek supper.

# Fisherman's pie

**For the topping**
625g (1lb 6oz) potatoes, washed, peeled, and cut into pieces
salt and freshly ground black pepper
4 tbsp milk
60g (2oz) butter

**For the filling**
1 litre (1¾ pints) milk
10 peppercorns
2 bay leaves
1 small onion, peeled and quartered
750g (1lb 10oz) skinned haddock fillets, cut into pieces
90g (3oz) butter, plus extra for greasing
60g (2oz) plain flour
leaves from 5–7 parsley sprigs, chopped
125g (4½oz) prawns, peeled, deveined, and cooked
3 eggs, hard-boiled, coarsely chopped

**1** Cook the potatoes in boiling, salted water for 15–20 minutes until tender. Drain, then return to the pan and mash. Heat the milk in a small pan, add the butter, salt, and black pepper. Stir and pour onto the mashed potatoes. Beat over a medium heat for 2–3 minutes, until potatoes are fluffy. Taste for seasoning. Set aside.

**2** For the filling, pour milk into a pan, then add the peppercorns, bay leaves, and onion. Bring to the boil, then remove from heat , cover, and leave to infuse for about 10 minutes. Add the fish, cover, and simmer for 5–10 minutes, until fish flakes easily when tested with a fork. Lift fish to a large plate and flake with a fork. Reserve the cooking liquid.

**3** Melt the butter in a pan. Whisk in the flour and cook until foaming. Remove from the heat. Pour the fish cooking liquid through a sieve and whisk into the flour and butter mixture. Return to the heat and cook, whisking, until the sauce boils and thickens. Season and simmer for 2 minutes. Stir in the parsley.

**4** Preheat the oven to 180°C (350°F/Gas 4). Melt some butter and use to brush a 2 litre (3½ pint) pie dish. Ladle one-third of the sauce into the dish. Spoon the flaked fish on top. Cover with the remaining sauce, then distribute the prawns on top. Sprinkle the chopped eggs over the prawns.Spread the mashed potatoes on top to cover filling completely. Bake for 20–30 minutes until the topping is brown and the sauce bubbles.

**SERVES** 6    **PREP** 20–30 MINS **COOK** 50 MINS – 1 HOUR PLUS INFUSING

When you need a simple yet sophisticated dish for entertaining, these individual pies are just the thing. Most fillings could be presented like this, just cut the lids to fit and bake until puffed up and golden.

# Chicken pot pies

**For the pastry**
350g (12oz) plain flour,
    plus extra for dusting
175g (6oz) butter, cubed
½ tsp salt
1 egg, beaten, to glaze

**For the filling**
1 litre (1¾ pints) chicken stock
3 carrots, sliced
750g (1lb 10oz) large potatoes, diced
3 celery sticks, thinly sliced

175g (6oz) peas
500g (1lb 2oz) cooked, skinless,
    boneless chicken, cut into slivers
60g (2oz) unsalted butter
1 onion, chopped
30g (1oz) plain flour
175ml (6fl oz) double cream
whole nutmeg, for grating
sea salt and freshly ground black pepper
leaves from 1 small bunch
    of parsley, chopped

**1** Preheat the oven to 200°C (400°F/Gas 6). To make the pastry, rub the flour and butter together until the mixture resembles breadcrumbs. Add salt and enough cold water to form a soft dough. Wrap in cling film and chill in the refrigerator for 30 minutes.

**2** For the filling, boil the stock in a large saucepan. Add the carrots, potatoes, and celery, and simmer for 3 minutes. Add the peas and simmer for 5 minutes until the vegetables are tender. Drain, reserving the stock. Put the chicken in a bowl and add the vegetables.

**3** Melt the butter in over a medium heat. Add the onion and cook until soft but not browned. Sprinkle over the flour and cook for 1–2 minutes, stirring. Add 500ml (16fl oz) stock and heat, whisking, until the sauce boils and thickens. Reduce the heat and simmer for 2 minutes. Add the cream, a grating of nutmeg, and seasoning. Pour over chicken and vegetables, and stir n the parsley. Divide filling evenly among 6 7.5cm (3in) round pie dishes.

**4** Roll out pastry to 5mm (¼in) thick. Use a 7.5cm (3in) cutter to cut out 6 rounds. Brush edge of pie dishes with water. Place a pastry round on top, pressing down to secure. Place pies on a baking tray, cut a slit in the top, brush with the beaten egg, and bake for 15–20 minutes.

**SERVES** 6     **PREP** 20 MINS PLUS CHILLING **COOK** 40 MINS     **FREEZE** UP TO 1 MONTH

A lovely recipe to cook from scratch, this pie is also a great time-saver. Cook double the amount of chicken, then before you debone it, simply freeze what you don't need for a delicious stew for another day.

# Coq au vin pie

**For the filling**
100g (3½oz) lardons
5 shallots, halved
2 garlic cloves, finely chopped
150g (5½oz) button mushrooms
4 chicken thighs
300ml (10fl oz) red wine
1 bay leaf

leaves from 4 sprigs of fresh thyme
   or ½ tsp dried thyme
salt and freshly ground black pepper
3 tbsp curly parsley, chopped

**For the pastry**
215g (7½oz) sheet ready-rolled puff pastry
   (or to make your own, see pp236–9)
1 egg, beaten, to glaze

**1** Heat a heavy-based saucepan, add lardons, and gently fry for 1 minute. Add the shallots and cook for 2 minutes. Add the garlic and mushrooms and cook for a further 1–2 minutes.

**2** Add the chicken, wine, bay leaf, and thyme to the pan, bring to the boil, season with salt and black pepper, cover, and simmer for 25 minutes or until chicken is tender and cooked.

**3** Place a colander over a large bowl or jug and tip contents of the pan into the colander. Set aside for 10 minutes to let all the juices to drain through and for the chicken to cool a little.

**4** Remove the bay leaf from the colander. Place the chicken on a plate and spoon the lardon and mushroom mixture into a 23cm (9in) pie dish. Remove the meat from the chicken pieces and add to the dish. Sprinkle the parsley over the filling.

**5** Return the drained cooking liquid to the pan, bring to the boil and cook over a high heat for 5–10 minutes to reduce and thicken. Pour the reduced sauce over the pie filling.

**6** Preheat the oven to 200°C (400°C/Gas 6). Cut enough 2cm (¾in) wide strips from the edge of the pastry to fit around the rim of the pie dish. Brush the edge of the dish with water and place the strips on the rim. Cover the pie with the remaining pastry, trim, and press firmly to seal. Brush with beaten egg and cut a slit in the top to allow steam to escape. Bake on a baking tray for 20–25 minutes or until browned.

**SERVES** 4–6   **PREP** 25 MINS PLUS COOLING   **FREEZE** UP TO 1 MONTH
**COOK** 55 MINS – 1 HOUR

Although often used to top sweet dishes, a cobbler topping can also be used to turn a stew or casserole into a one-pot meal. Add mustard, chopped herbs, or even horseradish to complement the filling.

# Chicken cobbler

**For the filling**

3 tbsp olive oil
1 onion, finely chopped
salt and freshly ground black pepper
3 garlic cloves, finely chopped
3 parsnips, peeled and sliced
6 chicken thighs, with skin on
1 tbsp plain flour, seasoned with salt
   and black pepper
120ml (4fl oz) Marsala wine, sherry,
   or white wine

a few tarragon leaves
about 450ml (15fl oz) hot chicken stock

**For the cobbler topping**

125g (4½oz) plain flour, sifted
salt and freshly ground black pepper
50g (1¾oz) butter, softened
25g (scant 1oz) Cheddar cheese, grated
3–4 tbsp buttermilk

**1** Preheat the oven to 150°C (300°F/Gas 2). Heat 1 tbsp of the olive oil in a large flameproof casserole over a medium heat. Add the onion and cook for 3–4 minutes until soft. Season with salt and black pepper, then stir in the garlic and parsnips, and cook for a further 2–3 minutes until the parsnips take on some colour. Remove the vegetables and set aside. Heat the remaining oil in the casserole over a higher heat.

**2** Toss the chicken in the flour and cook, skin-side down, for 8–10 minutes, or until golden all over. Pour in the Marsala and bring to the boil, then return the onion and parsnips to the casserole, add the tarragon, and pour over the stock. Bring to the boil, reduce to a simmer, cover with the lid, and put in the oven for 2 hours. Check occasionally that it's not drying out, topping up with a little hot water if needed.

**3** To make the cobbler topping, put the sifted flour into a bowl, season, then rub in the butter until the mixture resembles fine breadcrumbs. Stir in the cheese and add the buttermilk to form a dough. Roll out the dough on a lightly floured surface to 2.5cm (1in) thick and cut out 10 x 5cm (2in) diameter circles. For the last 30 minutes of cooking, place them around the edge of the stew and return to the oven, uncovered.

**SERVES** 4     **PREP** 20 MINS **COOK** 2½ HOURS

This tangy chicken pie is a pleasant change to a traditional pastry-based pie. Gently flavouring the filling with turmeric turns this midweek meal into something special.

# Vegetable and chicken pie

**For the topping**
450g (1lb) large potatoes, peeled
   and cut into large chunks
salt and freshly ground black pepper
a large knob of butter
4–5 tbsp milk

**For the filling**
40g (1½oz) butter
1 red pepper, thinly sliced

1 leek, sliced
¼ tsp ground turmeric
40g (1½oz) plain flour
250ml (9fl oz) milk
200g (7oz) tub crème fraîche
150g (5½oz) green beans, cut into 2cm (¾in)
   pieces and blanched
225g (8oz) cooked chicken, sliced
   (or 2–3 chicken thigh fillets, cooked)

**1** Preheat the oven to 200°C (400°F/Gas 6). Cook the potatoes in a large saucepan of boiling salted water for 15 minutes, or until tender. Drain, return the potatoes to the pan, and mash with the butter and enough milk to make a thick mash. Season with salt and set aside.

**2** For the filling, melt the butter in a large pan. Add the red pepper and leek, and cook for 3–4 minutes until soft. Stir in the turmeric, cook for a minute, then add the flour and cook for a further 2–3 minutes. Pour in the milk slowly, while stirring constantly, and cook for 4–5 minutes until thickened. Add the crème fraîche, green beans, and cooked chicken, and mix well.

**3** Season well with salt and black pepper and pour the filling into an overproof dish. Cover with the mashed potato, then cook in the oven for 25 minutes until hot.

**SERVES** 2   **PREP** 20 MINS **COOK** 50 MINS

A sophisticated pairing of wild mushrooms and cream perfectly complements the subtle gamey flavour of the guinea fowl. Serve with greens and plenty of mashed potato for a homely autumnal treat.

# Creamy wild mushroom and guinea fowl pie

**For the filling**

25g (scant 1oz) dried porcini mushrooms
1 tbsp olive oil
4 shallots, halved
2 garlic cloves, finely chopped
400g (14oz) guinea fowl breasts,
    cut into bite-sized pieces
200g (7oz) chestnut mushrooms, halved
2 tbsp Madeira

leaves from 1 bunch fresh thyme
    or 1 tsp dried thyme
¼ tsp freshly grated nutmeg
salt and freshly ground black pepper
2 tbsp double cream

**For the pastry**

215g (7½oz) sheet ready-rolled puff pastry
    (or to make your own, see pp236–9)
1 egg, beaten, to glaze

**1** Preheat the oven to 200°C (400°C/Gas 6). Place the porcini mushrooms in a small bowl and cover with boiling water. Set aside for 10 minutes, then drain and squeeze any moisture out of the mushrooms.

**2** Heat the olive oil in a medium, non-stick frying pan and gently fry the shallots for 3 minutes. Add the garlic and cook for 1–2 minutes.

**3** Add the guinea fowl and cook for 3–4 minutes until lightly browned. Add the chestnut mushrooms, porcini mushrooms, Madeira, thyme, nutmeg, and seasoning and cook gently for 5 minutes. Add the cream, stir well, and transfer to a 23cm (9in) pie dish.

**4** Cut enough 2cm (¾in) wide strips from the edge of the pastry to fit around the rim of the pie dish. Brush the edge of the dish with water and place the strips on the rim. Cover the pie with the remaining pastry, trim off the excess, and press firmly to seal. Brush with the beaten egg and cut a hole in the lid to allow steam to escape. Place on a baking tray and bake for 15–20 minutes until browned.

**SERVES** 6–8   **PREP** 25 MINS   **COOK** 30-35 MINS   **FREEZE** UP TO 1 MONTH

Mixing chopped fresh herbs into the pastry is an easy way of varying the flavours of a dish to complement the pie filling. Use farmed rabbit if possible here, as wild rabbit needs a long, slow cooking time.

# Rabbit with sweetcorn pie

**For the pastry**
345g (12oz) flour, plus extra for dusting
salt and freshly ground black pepper
175g (6oz) butter, chilled and diced
2 tbsp chopped parsley
1 tbsp chopped thyme

**For the filling**
1 oven-ready wild rabbit, jointed
60g (2oz) smoked bacon lardons

1 onion, chopped
2 carrots, sliced
1 potato, diced
4 tomatoes, skinned and chopped
kernels from 2 sweetcorn cobs
600ml (1 pint) chicken stock
1 bay leaf
3 tbsp dry sherry
4 tbsp double cream, plus extra to glaze

**1** To make the pastry, sift 225g (8oz) flour and ¼ tsp salt into a bowl. Add 60g (2oz) of the butter and rub in with your fingertips. Stir in the herbs. Add the remaining butter and 8 tbsp iced water and mix with a round-bladed knife to form a lumpy dough. On a floured surface, knead the dough, then roll out to an oblong. Fold the bottom-third up and the top-third down over it and press the edges with the rolling pin. Quarter-turn the dough then roll, fold, and turn twice more. Wrap in foil and chill for 30 minutes.

**2** For the filling, put the rabbit in a pan with the lardons and all the vegetables. Add the stock and bay leaf, and season. Bring to the boil, part-cover, and simmer for 1 hour until rabbit is tender. Remove the bay leaf, and lift out the rabbit. Remove the meat, cut into pieces, and put in a 1.7 litre (3 pint) pie dish on a baking tray. Blend sherry with remaining flour and 1 tbsp water. Stir into the vegetables and stock, Bring to the boil, stirring. Add cream, season and stir into the rabbit. Let cool. Preheat the oven to 220ºC (425ºF/Gas 7).

**3** Roll and fold the pastry once more then roll out to just bigger than the pie dish. Cut off a strip all round. Dampen the rim of the dish and lay the strip on top. Dampen the strip and lay the pastry on top. Press the edges together to seal. Trim, knock up, and flute with the back of a knife. Make leaves out of the trimmings and arrange on top. Cut a slit in the top and glaze with cream. Bake for 30 minutes until golden. Serve hot.

**SERVES** 4    **PREP** 40 MINS PLUS CHILLING **COOK** 1¾ HOURS    **FREEZE** UP TO 1 MONTH

This is an interpretation of the classic Moroccan pastilla, but here a large family-sized pie is served, which tastes even better cold.

# Guinea fowl pie

**For the filling**
1 small guinea fowl,
2 onions, quartered
4 garlic cloves, peeled
2cm (¾in) piece of ginger,
    thickly sliced
1 cinnamon stick
1 litre (1¾ pints) good-quality
    chicken stock
2 tbsp pomegranate molasses
1 tbsp runny honey
2 eggs, lightly beaten

2–3 heaped tbsp coriander, chopped
salt and freshly ground black pepper
100g (3½oz) walnut pieces, toasted
    and roughly chopped
50g (1¾oz) dried apricots,
    finely chopped
½ tsp ground cinnamon

**For the pastry**
3 tbsp olive oil
9 sheets ready-made filo pastry
icing sugar (optional)

**1** Remove guinea fowl breasts and set aside to use in another dish. Take legs and wings off and chop the carcass roughly. Put in a large pan. Add the onions, garlic, ginger, and cinnamon stick and cover with the stock. Bring to the boil, reduce the heat and simmer, uncovered, for 45 minutes, until the legs are cooked. Let cool, then strain through a colander, reserving the liquid. Clean the pan, add reserved liquid and boil until it just covers the base of the pan.

**2** Pull meat off the bones, leaving it in bite-sized shreds. Chop onions and garlic, and return to the pan with the meat. Mix in pomegranate molasses and honey and cook over a medium heat until mixture looks wet. Add eggs and coriander and cook for 2 minutes. Season and cool.

**3** Combine walnuts, apricots, and cinnamon. Preheat the oven to 190°C (375°F/Gas 5). Lightly grease the base of a 20cm (8in) springform cake tin with olive oil. Put a sheet of filo in the tin. Brush with more oil and layer a filo sheet on top, angling it slightly off centre to first piece. Repeat until you have used 6 layers. Spread half walnut mix over the base. Cover with half the meat. Top with remaining nut mix and finish with meat. Fold ragged edges over the top, cut the remaining filo in half, and repeat the layering process. Brush with oil. Bake for 30–40 minutes until brown. Cool for 5 minutes; dust with icing sugar, if liked.

**SERVES** 4 • **PREP** 1½ HOURS **COOK** 1½ HOURS • **FREEZE** FILLING UP TO 1 MONTH

After a festive meal there are sometimes more leftovers than you know what to do with. These little parcels make use of some of those leftovers, and are a good stand-by to serve unexpected guests.

# Roast turkey and cranberry turnovers

**For the pastry**
300g (10oz) plain flour,
   plus extra for dusting
150g (5½oz) butter, chilled and diced
½ tsp salt
1 egg, beaten, to glaze

**For the filling**
1 tbsp olive oil
1 red onion, finely chopped
2 garlic cloves, finely chopped
100ml (3½fl oz) half-fat crème fraîche
3 tbsp cranberry sauce
200g (7oz) roast turkey,
   roughly chopped
2 tbsp fresh, chopped
   or 1 tsp dried oregano
salt and freshly ground black pepper

**1** To make the pastry, rub the flour and butter together with your fingertips until the mixture resembles breadcrumbs. Add the salt and enough cold water to bring the mixture together to form a soft dough. Wrap in cling film and chill for 30 minutes.

**2** For the filling, heat olive oil in a frying pan. Add onion and cook on a medium heat for 3 minutes. Add garlic and cook for a further 2 minutes. Remove from the heat and stir in the crème fraîche, cranberry sauce, turkey, and oregano. Season well, and set aside.

**3** Preheat the oven to 190°C (375°F/Gas 5). Line 2 baking trays with baking parchment. Roll out the pastry on a floured surface to 5mm (¼in) thick. Using a 20cm (8in) diameter plate, cut out 4 circles from the dough, re-rolling pastry if necessary. Arrange one-quarter of the filling on half of each circle, leaving a 1cm (½in) border around the edge. Brush edges with beaten egg, then bring together to seal. Crimp for a decorative finish.

**4** Place the turnovers on prepared baking trays and brush with the remaining egg. Cut a slit in the top of each pastry for steam to escape and bake for 20–25 minutes until golden.

⊘ **SERVES** 4     ⏱ **PREP** 25 MINS PLUS CHILLING **COOK** 25-30 MINS     ❄ **FREEZE** UP TO 1 MONTH

A perfect dish for autumnal entertaining, this delicious steak pie is both homely and extravagant. If you can't find fresh wild mushrooms, use dried, or even dark chestnut mushrooms instead.

# Steak and wild mushroom pie

**For the filling**
500g (1lb 2oz) mixed wild mushrooms,
fresh, or 75g (2½oz) dried wild mushrooms,
   soaked for 30 minutes and drained
35g (1oz) plain flour
salt and freshly ground black pepper
1kg (2¼lb) braising steak,
   cut into 2.5cm (1in) cubes
4 shallots, finely chopped

900ml (1½ pints) beef stock
   or water, plus extra if needed
leaves from 6 sprigs of parsley,
finely chopped

**For the pastry**
215g (7½oz) sheet ready-rolled puff pastry
   (or to make your own, see pp236–9)
1 egg, beaten, to glaze

**1** Preheat the oven to 180°C (350°F/Gas 4). Slice the mushrooms. Make the filling by seasoning the flour with salt and black pepper. Toss the steak in it to coat.

**2** Put the meat, mushrooms, and shallots in an ovenproof casserole. Add the stock and heat, stirring well. Bring to the boil, stirring constantly. Cover, then cook in the oven for 2–2¼ hours until the meat is tender. Stir in the parsley and season. Spoon filling into a 23cm (9in) pie dish. Set aside to cool. This filling can be made 2–3 days ahead.

**3**. Increase the oven heat to 220°C (425°F/Gas 7). Cut enough 2cm (¾in) wide strips from the edge of the pastry to fit around the rim of the pie dish Dampen the rim of the pie dish and press the pastry strips onto it. Cover the pie with the remaining pastry, trim off the excess, and press firmly around the edge to seal. Brush with the beaten egg, cut a hole in the top and add a pie funnel to allow steam to escape. Chill for 15 minutes. Place on a baking tray and bake for 25–35 minutes until golden brown. If pie is browning too quickly, cover it with foil.

**SERVES** 4–6  **PREP** 50–55 MINS PLUS CHILLING  **FREEZE** UP TO 1 MONTH
**COOK** 2½–3 HOURS

Most cobblers rise like scones on baking. However, if you use plain flour, the topping will be thinner and have a crisper texture.

# Beef, fennel, and mushroom cobbler

**For the filling**
1kg (2½lb) stewing beef,
   cut into bite-sized pieces
salt and freshly ground black pepper
1 tbsp plain flour
2 tsp mild paprika
3 tbsp olive oil
2 onions, finely sliced
3 fennel bulbs, trimmed and cut into eighths
150ml (5fl oz) dry white wine
1.2 litres (2 pints) hot beef stock
   or vegetable stock

a knob of butter
450g (1lb) chestnut mushrooms, quartered
a pinch of dried oregano

**for the cobbler topping**
150g (5½oz) each plain flour and cornmeal,
   plus extra for dusting
50g (1¾oz) butter
90ml (3fl oz) milk
1 egg yolk, beaten, to glaze

**1** Preheat the oven to 180°C (350°F/Gas 4). Season meat, place in a bowl, and toss with flour and paprika until evenly coated. Heat half the olive oil in a large ovenproof pan, add meat, and cook over a medium heat until evenly browned. Brown meat in batches as there is too much to cook altogether. Remove with a slotted spoon and set aside.

**2** Heat the remaining oil in the pan. Add the onions and cook until soft. Season well. Add the fennel and cook until beginning to soften. Add wine, increase heat, and simmer for 1–2 minutes until alcohol evaporates. Return meat to the pan, pour in the stock, and bring to the boil. Cover and bake in the oven for 1 hour.

**3** To make topping, rub flour, cornmeal, a pinch of salt, and the butter together until mixture resembles breadcrumbs. Stir in enough milk to form a soft dough. Chill for 20 minutes. Roll out on a floured surface and cut out 16 circles with a 6cm (2½in) cutter.

**4** When meat has been cooking for 1 hour, melt butter in a frying pan. Add mushrooms and oregano, and cook until soft. Stir into the beef and fennel and cook for a further 30 minutes. Increase oven temperature to 200°C (400°F/Gas 6). Top the stew with cobbler circles, overlapping them. Brush with egg and bake for 30–40 minutes until golden.

**SERVES** 8    **PREP** 20 MINS PLUS CHILLING    **FREEZE** UP TO 2 MONTHS
**COOK** 2½ HOURS                                FILLING ONLY

These tasty meat and potato hand pies were originally created as a portable meal for field workers to carry with them. The thick-pleated crust was used as a handle for dirty hands, and discarded after use.

# Cornish pasties

**For the pastry**
100g (3½oz) lard, chilled and diced
50g (1¾oz) unsalted butter,
    chilled and diced
300g (10oz) plain flour
    plus extra for dusting
½ tsp salt
1 egg, beaten, to glaze

**For the filling**
250g (9oz) beef skirt, trimmed and
    cut into 1cm (½in) cubes
80g (2¾oz) swede, peeled and
    cut into 5mm (¼in) cubes
100g (3½oz) waxy potatoes, peeled
    and cut into 5mm (¼in) cubes
1 large onion, finely chopped
splash of Worcestershire sauce
1 tsp plain flour
sea salt and freshly ground black pepper

**1** To make the pastry, rub the lard and butter into the flour until the mixture resembles fine breadcrumbs. Add the salt and enough cold water to form a soft dough. On a floured surface, knead dough briefly, then wrap in cling film and chill for 30 minutes.

**2** Preheat the oven to 190°C (375°F/Gas 5). Mix all the filling ingredients together and season well with salt and black pepper.

**3** Roll out pastry on a well-floured surface to 5mm (¼in) thick. Using a side plate, or saucer, cut 4 circles from the dough. Re-roll the offcuts. Fold the circles in half, then flatten them out, leaving a slight mark down the centre. Pile one-quarter of the filling into each circle, leaving a 2cm (¾in) border all around.

**4** Brush the border of the pastry with a little beaten egg. Pull both edges up over filling and press together to seal. Crimp the sealed edge with your fingers to form a decorative ridge along the top. Brush a little beaten egg all over the finished pasties. Place on a baking tray.

**5** Bake in the middle of the oven for 40–45 minutes until golden brown. Set the pasties aside to cool for at least 15 minutes before eating. Serve warm or cold.

**SERVES** 4    **PREP** 20 MINS PLUS CHILLING **COOK** 40–45 MINS    **FREEZE** UP TO 1 MONTH

This classic French pie was originally designed to use up leftover roast beef, but is more commonly made using fresh minced beef.

# Beef and herb potato pie

**For the filling**
4 garlic cloves, peeled
75ml (2½fl oz) olive oil,
   plus extra for greasing
1 large onion, diced
1kg (2¼lb) minced beef
salt and freshly ground black pepper
400g can chopped tomatoes
250ml (9fl oz) beef stock
125ml (4fl oz) dry white wine

**For the topping**
1kg (2¼lb) potatoes, peeled
   and cut into 2–3 pieces
salt and freshly ground black pepper
1 bunch of basil, leaves only
1 bunch of parsley, leaves only
250ml (9fl oz) milk,
   plus extra if needed

**1** Finely chop 2 garlic cloves. Heat one-third of the olive oil in a frying pan. Add the onion and cook for 3–5 minutes, stirring, until soft. Add the chopped garlic, minced beef, salt, black pepper, and tomatoes. Reduce heat and cook gently, stirring occasionally, for 10–12 minutes, until the meat is brown. Stir in the stock and wine. Simmer over a very low heat for 25–30 minutes, stirring occasionally, until most of the liquid has evaporated, but the meat is still moist. Do not cook the meat too fast or it will be tough.

**2** To make the topping, place the potatoes in a pan with plenty of cold water. Add salt, cover and bring to the boil. Reduce heat and simmer for 15–20 minutes, until tender. Blitz the basil, parsley leaves, and the rest of the garlic with the remaining oil in a food processor to form a purée, scraping the side of the bowl occasionally.

**3** Drain the potatoes, return them to the pan and mash. Add the herb purée. Scald the milk in another pan. Gradually beat the milk into the potatoes over a medium heat, and stir for 2–3 minutes, until the potatoes just hold a shape. Season to taste.

**4** Preheat the oven to 190°C (375°F/Gas 5). Grease a large shallow baking dish. Check meat for seasoning, then spoon, with any liquid, into the dish. Spoon over an even layer of potatoes and smooth top with the back of a spoon. Make a scalloped pattern on the potatoes. Bake for 35–40 minutes, until golden brown, with gravy bubbling at the edges.

**SERVES** 6    **PREP** 25–30 MINS **COOK** 2–2½ HOURS

The unusual addition of a little ketchup in the pastry here gives the crust extra flavour. This family-sized pie is perfect for those times when you want to prepare a special picnic or garden meal.

# Sausage, bacon, and egg pie

**For the pastry**
350g (12oz) plain flour,
  plus extra for dusting
175g (6oz) butter
salt and freshly ground black pepper
1½ tbsp tomato ketchup

**For the filling**
450g (1lb) sausagemeat
  or good-quality pork sausages, skinned
½ onion, finely chopped
a pinch of nutmeg
a pinch of mace
1 tbsp wholegrain mustard
6 streaky, rindless bacon bashers
4 eggs
milk, to glaze

**1** To make the pastry, rub the butter into the flour with your fingertips until the mixture resembles breadcrumbs. Season with salt and black pepper, then add the ketchup and enough cold water for the mixture to form a soft dough. Wrap the dough in cling film and chill in the refrigerator for 30 minutes.

**2** Preheat the oven to 200°C (400°F/Gas 6). Roll out half of the pastry fairly thinly on a lightly floured surface and use to line a greased 20cm (8in), 3.5cm (1½in) deep pie dish.

**3** To make the filling, mix the sausagemeat with the onion, nutmeg, mace, and mustard. Season to taste and spread evenly over the bottom of the pastry-lined pie dish. Place the bacon over the sausagemeat in lines and crack the eggs over the bacon, leaving them intact if possible, as it looks nice when slicing the pie.

**4** Roll out the remaining pastry and use to cover the pie, then pinch the edges firmly with your thumb and forefinger to seal. Lightly score a criss-cross pattern on top of the pie and brush with a little milk.

**5** Bake the pie for 20 minutes, then reduce the heat to 180°C (350°F/Gas 4), and bake for a further 30 minutes. Cool before serving.

**SERVES** 6–8    **PREP** 15 MINS PLUS CHILLING **COOK** 50 MINS

A meaty pie with a crisp, buttery pastry top is always a welcome sight at the kitchen table. Using apple juice here sweetens and mellows the tasty filling to create a real winter classic.

# Pork and leek pie

**For the filling**
2 tbsp vegetable oil
450g (1lb) lean boneless pork steaks,
    cut into 2.5cm (1in) cubes
2 leeks, thickly sliced
150g (5½oz) mushrooms, halved
1 tsp thyme leaves
150ml (5fl oz) chicken stock
1 tbsp cornflour, mixed with 1 tbsp water

250ml (9fl oz) apple juice
2 tbsp tomato purée
salt and freshly ground black pepper

**For the pastry**
plain flour, for dusting
250g (9oz) ready-made shortcrust pastry
    (or to make your own, see p228)
1 egg, beaten, to glaze

**1** Heat the vegetable oil in a frying pan, add the pork and fry until browned, then remove from the pan and set aside. Add the leeks, mushrooms and thyme to the pan and fry for 5 minutes. Add the stock, cornflour, apple juice and tomato purée, and bring to the boil, stirring until thickened. Return the pork to the pan, season to taste, and simmer for 25 minutes.

**2** Transfer the pork and vegetables to an 18cm (7in) round pie dish, reserving the sauce. On a lightly floured surface, roll out the pastry and use to cover the dish, decorating the top with the pastry trimmings. Cut a slit in the top of the pie to allow the steam to escape, then brush all over with the beaten egg. Chill for 30 minutes.

**3** Preheat the oven to 200°C (400°F/Gas 6). Bake the pie for 35 minutes, or until the pastry is golden, then serve with the warmed reserved sauce.

**SERVES** 4     **PREP** 25 MINS PLUS CHILLING **COOK** 1 HOUR 10 MINS     **FREEZE** UP TO 1 MONTH

This picnic pie makes a fabulous centrepiece for a summer buffet. Making it the old-fashioned way, using lard in the pastry, helps keep the crust fresh for days, but sturdy enough to hold the filling.

# Pork and apple picnic pie

**For the pastry**
400g (14oz) plain flour,
   plus extra for dusting
150g (5½oz) lard
1 tsp salt

**For the filling**
1 tbsp olive oil
1 onion, finely chopped
100g (3½oz) pancetta,
   finely chopped

500g (1lb 2oz) minced pork
2 dessert apples, peeled,
   cored, and grated
2 tbsp apple juice
¼ tsp nutmeg, grated
1 tbsp sage or flat-leaf parsley,
   finely chopped
salt and freshly ground black pepper
1 egg yolk, beaten with
   1 tsp cold water, to glaze

**1** To make the pastry, rub the flour, lard, and salt together until the mixture resembles breadcrumbs. Add 6–8 tablespoons cold water, a little at a time, and bring together to form a dough. Add a little extra water, if needed. Wrap and chill for 30 minutes.

**2** For the filling, heat olive oil in a frying pan and fry onion and pancetta for 5 minutes until soft, then set aside to cool. Mix the pork, apples, apple juice, nutmeg, herbs, and lots of salt and black pepper together in a large bowl, then mix in the onion mixture.

**3** Preheat the oven to 190°C (375°F/Gas 5). Roll out pastry on a floured surface into a large circle about 7mm (¼in) thick. Use to line a greased 22cm (9in) loose-bottomed tart tin, making sure it overlaps the sides. Trim all but 1cm (½in) of the overhanging pastry.

**4** Pile the filling into the tart case pressing it down firmly. Roll out the remaining piece of pastry to make a circle large enough to cover the pie. Brush the edges with a little of the egg mixture, place the top on the pie, and press down firmly to seal. Crimp the edges. Brush top with the remaining egg and poke 2 small holes in the top of the pie.

**5** Place the pie on a baking tray and bake for 1 hour until golden. Set pie aside to cool completely before serving. It can be stored in a refrigerator, wrapped, for up to 3 days.

**SERVES** 8      **PREP** 30 MINS PLUS CHILLING **COOK** 1 HOUR

# puddings

Also known as *Arroz doce*, this is a traditional Portuguese dessert. Use full-fat milk as it will work far better. The eggs will cook in the residual heat. It is also good sprinkled with ground cinnamon

# Chocolate rice pudding

500g (1lb 2oz) short-grain rice
1 tsp salt
1.2 litres (2 pints) full-fat milk
1 tbsp cocoa powder
250g (9oz) caster sugar
6 egg yolks
4 tbsp grated dark chocolate

**1** Bring 2 litres (3½ pints) water to the boil in a large saucepan. Add the rice and salt and bring back to the boil. Reduce the heat, cover, and cook for 10 minutes, then drain.

**2** Pour the milk into a saucepan and add the cocoa. Bring to the boil, then add the rice. Reduce the heat and cook, uncovered, for 30 minutes or until the rice is soft. Add the sugar and stir until dissolved, then remove from the heat and quickly beat in the egg yolks.

**3** Divide the rice between individual serving dishes, level the tops, and sprinkle with the grated chocolate. Leave to cool, then serve.

**SERVES** 4–6    **PREP** 10 MINS **COOK** 40 MINS

This sweet, creamy, and very rich dessert is a popular party dish in Brazil where it is known as *Quindim*. It needs to be made ahead so it has plenty of time to chill in the refrigerator.

# Brazilian baked custards with coconut

100g (3½oz) caster sugar
4 egg yolks
2 tbsp grated fresh coconut or dessicated
   coconut, plus extra, toasted, to serve
60ml (2fl oz) coconut milk

**1** Preheat the oven to 180°C (350°F/Gas 4). Whisk the sugar and egg yolks in a bowl until light and creamy. Add the grated or dessicated coconut and coconut milk and stir until evenly combined. Spoon into 4 x 150ml (5fl oz) ramekins and cover each one with foil.

**2** Stand the ramekins in a roasting tin and pour in enough warm water to come halfway up the sides of the dishes. Put in the oven for 25–30 minutes until the custards are set. Carefully lift the dishes out of the tin, leave to cool, and then chill for at least 3–4 hours. Serve with the toasted coconut sprinkled on top.

**SERVES** 4     **PREP** 15 MINS PLUS CHILLING **COOK** 25-30 MINS

This is a delicious classic infused with the taste of vanilla. In this recipe, the seeds are discarded, but for something more aromatic, deseed the pod and add the seeds to the milk at the same time.

# Classic crème caramel

600ml (1 pint) full-fat milk
1 vanilla pod, split lengthways
   and deseeded
225g (8oz) golden caster sugar
2 whole eggs
4 egg yolks

**1** Preheat the oven to 150°C (300°F/Gas 2). Pour the milk into a heavy-based pan, add the vanilla pod, and very gently bring almost to the boil. Turn off the heat, cover the pan with the lid, and leave for 20 minutes. This is to give the vanilla pod time to infuse the milk while it cools.

**2** Add half of the sugar to another heavy-based pan, then pour in 75ml (2½fl oz) of cold water. Slowly bring to the boil, swirling it around the pan occasionally to ensure the sugar has dissolved, then boil for about 15 minutes, until the liquid turns a dark golden caramel. Pour this into 6 x 150ml (5fl oz) ramekins, or use larger ones if making fewer crème caramels.

**3** Put the remaining sugar with the eggs and egg yolks into a bowl and whisk until well combined and the sugar has dissolved. Discard the vanilla pod and pour the cooled milk into the egg mixture, then briefly whisk again and pour through a sieve into the ramekins. Sit the ramekins in a deep ovenproof dish, pour in boiling water to come two-thirds of the way up the sides of the ramekins, and cook for 1 hour. Remove the dish from the oven, leaving the ramekins in the hot water for 30 minutes to continue setting. Then leave to cool and chill overnight in the fridge. Turn out to serve.

**SERVES** 6    **PREP** 15 MINS PLUS INFUSING AND CHILLING **COOK** 1½ HOURS

Rich and decadent, these mini puddings are delicious served hot with some vanilla ice cream. To cook the puddings in one batch, use a pan that is a minimum of 4.5 litres (8 pints) in size.

# Chocolate and prune sponge puddings

125g (4½oz) butter, softened
125g (4½oz) caster sugar
2 eggs, beaten
125g (4½oz) self-raising flour, sifted
30g (1oz) cocoa powder, mixed
   with 2 tbsp milk
125g (4½oz) prunes, stoned
   and chopped

**1** Grease 6 x 150ml (5fl oz) metal pudding moulds. Put the butter and sugar into a mixing bowl and beat together until creamy and pale. Add the eggs slowly, beating as you go and adding a little flour to prevent any curdling. Then fold in the remaining flour until it is thoroughly combined, and stir through the cocoa mixture and prunes.

**2** Divide the mixture between the moulds and cover each one with a pleated piece of greased greaseproof paper and a sheet of foil, kept in place with string.

**3** Sit the moulds in a large heavy-based pan and pour in enough boiling water to come halfway up the sides of the pudding moulds. Cover with the lid and leave to simmer gently for about 45 minutes, topping up with more boiling water as and when needed. Carefully lift the moulds out of the pan, remove the string, foil, and paper, and turn out onto warmed plates. Serve hot with ice cream, cream, custard, or chocolate sauce.

**SERVES** 6    **PREP** 30–40 MINS **COOK** 45 MINS

Here is a light citrussy pudding that is best enjoyed with plenty of custard. You could add a small handful of chopped almonds to the mixture for added texture.

# Lemon sponge pudding

grated zest and juice of 2 lemons
juice of ½ large orange
60g (2oz) light soft brown sugar
115g (4oz) unsalted butter, softened
60g (2oz) caster sugar
1 tbsp golden syrup
2 eggs
175g (6oz) self-raising flour, sifted

**1** Grease a 1 litre (1¾ pint) pudding basin. Stir together the juice of 1 lemon with the orange juice and brown sugar in a bowl, and pour this into the pudding basin. Put the butter, caster sugar, and golden syrup into a mixing bowl along with the lemon zest and beat together until creamy and pale. Add the eggs slowly, beating as you go and adding a little flour to prevent any curdling. Then fold in the remaining flour until it is thoroughly combined, and stir through the remaining lemon juice.

**2** Pour the mixture into the basin and cover with a pleated piece of greased greaseproof paper and a sheet of foil. Secure with string, looping it around the basin to form a handle.

**3** Sit the pudding bowl in a large heavy-based pan and pour in enough boiling water to come halfway up the side of the basin. Cover with the lid and leave to simmer gently for about 1½ hours, topping up with more boiling water as and when needed. Carefully lift the basin out of the pan, remove the string, foil, and paper, and turn the pudding out onto a plate. Serve piping hot with custard or cream.

**SERVES** 4–6　**PREP** 30–40 MINS **COOK** 1½ HOURS

Steamed puddings do not have to be stodgy – this light version is a case in point and it's full of dried fruit and spices. For something a little simpler, use sultanas in place of the mixed dried fruit.

# Mixed fruit pudding

60g (2oz) butter, softened
60g (2oz) golden caster sugar
2 eggs, lightly beaten
85g (3oz) self-raising flour, sifted
100g (3½oz) mixed dried fruit
pinch of ground cinnamon
pinch of mixed spice
1 tbsp milk
1–2 tbsp golden syrup

**1** Lightly grease a 600ml (1 pint) pudding basin. Put the butter and sugar in a food mixer and beat until pale and creamy, or use a hand-held electric mixer.

**2** Add the eggs, a little at a time, with a little of the flour, beating gently as you go. Then add the remaining flour together with the fruit and spices and beat lightly. Finally, add the milk and stir until everything is combined.

**3** Put 1–2 tbsp of the golden syrup (depending on how sweet you like it) in the bottom of the pudding basin, then spoon the mixture into the basin. Cover with a pleated piece of greaseproof paper and a sheet of foil. Secure with string, looping it around the basin to form a handle. Sit the pudding basin in a large heavy-based pan and pour in enough boiling water to come halfway up the side of the basin. Cover with the lid and simmer gently for about 1½ hours, topping up with more boiling water if needed. Carefully remove the basin from the pan, remove the string, foil, and paper, and turn the pudding out onto a plate. Serve with cream or custard.

**SERVES** 4–6     **PREP** 15 MINS **COOK** 1¾ HOURS     **FREEZE** UP TO 3 MONTHS

For an even richer experience, consider using flavoured mint, ginger, or coffee chocolate. To cook the puddings in one batch, use a roasting tin that is at least 4.5 litres (8 pints) in size.

# Chocolate mousses

2 eggs
3 egg yolks
100g (3½oz) caster sugar
100g (3½oz) dark chocolate (70 per cent
   cocoa solids), broken into pieces
300ml (10fl oz) double cream

**1** Preheat the oven to 160°C (325°F/Gas 3) and grease 6 x 100ml (3½fl oz) ramekins or metal pudding basins. Put the eggs, egg yolks, and sugar in a mixing bowl and whisk until creamy. Set aside.

**2** Put the chocolate in a heatproof bowl and sit it over a pan of barely simmering water. Stir occasionally until melted, remove from the heat, and set aside. Heat the cream in a pan so it is warm, but do not boil, then slowly add the egg mixture, whisking as you go. Stir through the chocolate until it is very well combined.

**3** Pour the mixture into the prepared ramekins or basins, then sit them in a roasting tin and carefully pour hot water into the tin so it comes halfway up the sides of the ramekins. Sit in the oven and cook for 15–20 minutes; they should still have a wobble in them when they are ready. Remove from the oven and leave to cool, then transfer to the refrigerator for a couple of hours to chill. Turn out each mousse onto a bowl and serve with ice cream or shortbread biscuits.

**SERVES** 6     **PREP** 20 MINS **COOK** 30 MINS

You could change the cinnamon in these dumplings for grated nutmeg or mixed spice, and use orange zest instead of lemon for a slightly sweeter finish.

# Apple dumplings

225g (8oz) self-raising flour, sifted
115g (4oz) vegetable suet
1 tsp ground cinnamon, plus extra to serve
grated zest of 1 lemon
4 cooking apples, peeled and cored
1 tbsp demerara sugar
60g (2oz) golden sultanas
icing sugar, to serve

**1** Preheat the oven to 180°C (350°F/Gas 4) and lightly grease a baking tray. To make the suet pastry, put the flour, suet, cinnamon, and lemon zest into a bowl. Then slowly trickle in about 100ml (3½fl oz) of cold water and mix together until it forms a dough.

**2** Roll out the pastry and cut out 4 circles, large enough for each apple. Sit an apple on each round, sprinkle the demerara sugar into the apple holes, and add the sultanas to each. Brush the edges of the pastry with water and bring them together at the top, pinching to secure.

**3** Turn the apples over so the sealed side is face down. If you have any pastry left over, you could fashion leaves and stalks for the dumplings. Sit them on the baking tray. Cook in the oven for 30–40 minutes until golden. Sprinkle the dumplings with icing sugar and ground cinnamon and serve with cream, custard, or ice cream.

**SERVES** 4     **PREP** 20 MINS **COOK** 30-40 MINS

A classic comfort food, for many people apple pie is the taste of home. Butter can be used instead of lard in the pastry.

# Apple pie

**For the pastry**
330g (11oz) plain flour,
 plus extra for dusting
½ tsp salt
150g (5½oz) lard or white vegetable fat,
 plus extra for greasing
2 tbsp caster sugar,
 plus extra for sprinkling
1 tbsp milk, to glaze

**For the filling**
1kg (2¼lb) tart apples, peeled,
 quartered, and cored
juice of 1 lemon
2 tbsp plain flour
½ tsp ground cinnamon,
 or to taste
¼ tsp grated nutmeg,
 or to taste
100g (3½oz) caster sugar

**1** To make the pastry, sift flour and salt into a bowl. Add fat and rub into the flour with your fingertips until the mixture resembles breadcrumbs. Add sugar. Sprinkle with 6–7 tbsp cold water. Mix with a fork, then press into a ball. Wrap and chill for 30 minutes.

**2** Grease a 23cm (9in) shallow pie dish. On a floured surface, roll out two-thirds of the pastry into a circle, 5cm (2in) larger than the dish. Use to line the dish, gently push it into the contours. Trim any excess, then chill for 15 minutes until firm.

**3** Set apple quarters, cut-side down, on a chopping board and slice. Put in a bowl and pour on lemon juice. Sprinkle over the flour, cinnamon, nutmeg, and sugar and toss to coat. Arrange apples in the pie dish. Brush the edge of the pastry with water. Roll remaining pastry to a 28cm (11in) circle. Drape it over the filling and trim. Press the pastry edges together to seal, crimping with the back of a knife as you go.

**4** Cut an "x" in the top. Pull back point of each triangle to reveal filling. Roll out pastry trimmings, cut into strips, and moisten. Lay on pie in a criss-cross pattern. Brush top with the milk, sprinkle over sugar, and chill for 30 minutes. Preheat the oven to 220°C (425°F/Gas 7).

**5** Bake for 20 minutes. Reduce to 180°C (350°F/Gas 4) and bake for 30–35 minutes. Insert a skewer to check the apples are tender. Serve warm.

**SERVES** 6-8    **PREP** 30–35 MINS, PLUS CHILLING **COOK** 50-55 MINS    **FREEZE** UP TO 1 MONTH

Not strictly a pie, but a popular French "pie-like" classic, this recipe is great when eaten as a dessert, warm from the oven with thick cream, but will keep for several days to serve cold.

# Apple tourte with nuts and raisins

100g (3½oz) unsalted butter,
plus extra for greasing
100g (3½oz) caster sugar
1 tsp vanilla extract
2 eggs
150g (5½oz) self-raising flour
1 tsp ground cinnamon
2 dessert apples, peeled, cored,
  and finely sliced
30g (1oz) raisins
30g (1oz) walnuts, roughly chopped

**1** Preheat the oven to 180°C (350°F/Gas 4). Grease and line the bottom of a 20cm (8in) springform cake tin. Melt the butter and set aside to cool.

**2** Whisk the sugar, vanilla extract, and eggs together in a large bowl. Whisk in the cooled, melted butter until all the ingredients are thoroughly mixed. Sift in the flour and cinnamon, and fold together well. Finally, fold in the apples, raisins, and walnuts.

**3** Pour the mixture into the prepared cake tin and smooth the top. Bake for 30–35 minutes until is well risen and golden brown, and a skewer inserted into the centre comes out clean.

**4** Set the tourte aside to rest for at least 15 minutes before serving warm with whipped cream, or cold as a cake. Best eaten the same day, but can be stored, well wrapped, for up to 2 days.

⊙ **SERVES** 8     🕐 **PREP** 20 MINS **COOK** 30-35 MINS     ❄ **FREEZE** UP TO 2 MONTHS

A classic frangipane-filled tart, this recipe hails from Normandy in northern France where they grow the most wonderful pears. Best eaten warm or at room temperature the day it is made.

# Normandy pear tart

**For the pastry**
175g (6oz) plain flour
3 egg yolks
60g (2oz) caster sugar
a pinch of salt
75g (2½oz) unsalted butter, softened,
    plus extra for greasing
½ tsp vanilla extract

**For the filling**
125g (4½oz) whole blanched almonds
125g (4½oz) butter
100g (3½oz) sugar
1 egg, plus 1 egg yolk
3–5 tbsp Kirsch
3–4 pears, peeled, cored, and cut in wedges
juice of 1 lemon
150g (5½oz) apricot jam

**1** For the pastry, sift flour onto a work surface, make a well in the centre, add the egg yolks, sugar, salt, 75g (2½oz) butter, and vanilla and mix with your fingertips. Work the flour into the other ingredients until the mixture forms a soft dough. If too dry, add a little water. On a floured surface, knead for 1–2 minutes. Wrap in cling film and chill for 30 minutes. Grease a 23–25cm (9–10in) loose-bottomed, fluted tart tin. Roll out the pastry on a floured surface to a circle, 5cm (2in) larger than the tin, and use to line the tin. Prick the bottom with a fork. Chill for 15 minutes.

**2** Preheat the oven to 200°C (400°F/Gas 6). Grind the almonds to a "flour" in a food processor and set aside. Make the frangipane filling by beating together the butter and sugar until light and fluffy. Gradually add the egg and egg yolk, beating in well. Add 1 tbsp Kirsch, then gently stir in the ground almonds. Toss the pears with the lemon juice, and set aside. Spread frangipane over the pastry in the tin and arrange pears on top. Set the tin on a baking tray. Bake for 12–15 minutes. Reduce the heat to 180°C (350°F/Gas 4) and bake for 25–30 minutes until set. Melt the jam with the remaining Kirsch, and work the mixture through a sieve, then let cool slightly Unmould the pie and brush with the apricot glaze. Serve warm.

**SERVES** 6-8     **PREP** 40-45 MINS, PLUS CHILLING **COOK** 35-45 MINS     **FREEZE** UP TO 1 MONTH

Careful cooking at a low temperature will produce a pudding with a smooth, velvety texture – a perfect use for leftover white bread. For extra decadence, you could use brioche or croissants.

# Bread and butter pudding

30g (1oz) butter, plus extra to grease
5–6 slices of day-old bread, crusts removed,
   about 175g (6oz) total weight
60g (2oz) raisins
3 eggs
300ml (10fl oz) full-fat milk
200ml (7fl oz) single cream
60g (2oz) caster sugar
1 tsp pure vanilla extract
4 tbsp apricot jam
2–3 tsp lemon juice

**1** Lightly grease an ovenproof dish with a little butter. Spread the remaining butter on the slices of bread. Cut each slice in half diagonally, then in half again to form 4 triangles.

**2** Place the raisins in the bottom of the dish and arrange overlapping slices of bread across the top. Beat together the eggs, milk, cream, sugar, and vanilla extract. Carefully pour the mixture over the bread, cover with foil, and leave to soak for at least 30 minutes.

**3** Preheat the oven to 180°C (350°F/Gas 4). Place the dish in a deep roasting tin and pour boiling water into the tin to a depth of 2.5cm (1in). Bake in the oven for 30–40 minutes, until still slightly moist in the centre, but not runny.

**4** Meanwhile, put the jam in a small pan with the lemon juice and 1 tbsp water. Bring to the boil, then push the melted jam through a sieve. Carefully brush or spoon the sieved jam over the surface of the hot pudding to glaze. Serve with cream or custard.

**SERVES** 4    **PREP** 15 MINS, PLUS SOAKING **COOK** 40 MINS    **FREEZE** UP TO 3 MONTHS

Both the rice and the peaches can be prepared one day ahead and kept covered in the refrigerator. Let the rice come to room temperature, or warm it in a low oven, before serving.

# Creamy rice pudding with peaches

65g (2¼oz) short-grain rice
1 litre (1¾ pints) milk, plus
   more if needed
5cm (2in) cinnamon stick
50g (1¾oz) caster sugar
salt

**For the peaches**
4 ripe peaches, peeled, halved,
   stoned, and cut into wedges
60g (2oz) caster sugar, plus more
   if needed
250ml (9fl oz) dry red wine, plus
   more if needed

**1** To prepare the peaches, put them in a non-metallic bowl and sprinkle with the sugar; they may need more or less sugar than specified, depending on their sweetness. Pour over enough red wine to cover the fruit completely. Set a plate on top and leave to macerate in the refrigerator for at least 2 hours and up to 24 hours. Strain the liquid into a saucepan, bring to the boil, and simmer for 2 minutes until syrupy. Stir it back into the peaches.

**2** Preheat the oven to 150°C (300°F/Gas 2). Put the rice, milk, cinnamon stick, sugar, and a pinch of salt into an ovenproof dish and stir. Put it in the oven for 3 hours, uncovered, and stirring gently every 30 minutes until the pudding is thick and creamy. Cover the dish with foil if it starts to brown too much.

**3** Remove the pudding from the oven. Carefully slip a spoon down the side and stir from the bottom. Let it stand for 1 hour. Discard the cinnamon stick, ladle into serving bowls, and serve with the peaches and wine syrup, which can be either warmed or cold.

**SERVES** 4-6    **PREP** 15-20 MINS, PLUS MACERATING AND STANDING **COOK** 3 HOURS

Here the peaches are gently poached for a few minutes before assembling the cobbler, which helps to break them down on cooking. Really ripe, juicy peaches will need no such help.

# Peach cobbler

**For the filling**
50g (1¾oz) caster sugar
8 ripe peaches, peeled,
    stoned, and quartered
1 tsp cornflour
juice of ½ lemon

**For the cobbler topping**
225g (8oz) self-raising flour
2 tsp baking powder

75g (2½oz) caster sugar
pinch of salt
½–¾ tsp ground cinnamon, to taste
75g (2½oz) unsalted butter
1 egg
100ml (3fl oz) buttermilk
1 tbsp soft light brown sugar

**1** Preheat the oven to 190°C (375°F/Gas 5). For the filling, heat the sugar and 3–4 tbsp water in a large, heavy-based saucepan. Once the sugar has dissolved, add the quartered peaches, cover, and cook over a medium heat for 2–3 minutes.

**2** Mix the cornflour with the lemon juice to make a paste, then add it to the peaches. Continue to cook uncovered, over a low heat until the liquid thickens around the peaches. Transfer the peaches and syrup to a shallow ovenproof dish.

**3** To make the cobbler topping, sift the flour, baking powder, sugar, salt, and cinnamon into a large bowl. Rub in the butter with your fingertips until the mixture resembles fine breadcrumbs. Whisk together the egg and buttermilk in a separate bowl. Add the liquid to the dry ingredients and bring together to form a soft, sticky dough.

**4** Drop heaped tablespoons of the dough over the surface of the fruit, leaving a little space between them. Sprinkle with the brown sugar. Bake for 25–30 minutes until golden and bubbling. It is ready when a skewer inserted into the centre of the topping comes out clean. Set aside to cool for 5 minutes before serving with ice cream, custard, or cream.

**SERVES** 6-8    **PREP** 20 MINS **COOK** 30-35 MINS

This classic French tart is filled with a delicate custard and juicy apricots. Canned apricots are often more reliable than fresh ones, but if you have some ripe apricots do use them instead.

# Apricot tart

**For the pastry**
175g (6oz) plain flour,
   plus extra for dusting
25g (scant 1oz) caster sugar
100g (3½oz) unsalted butter,
   at room temperature, cut into pieces
1 egg yolk, beaten with 2 tbsp cold water,
   plus 1 egg white, for brushing

**For the filling**
200ml (7fl oz) double cream
50g (1¾oz) caster sugar
2 eggs, plus 1 egg yolk
½ tsp vanilla extract
400g tin apricot halves, drained
icing sugar, for dusting

**1** To make the pastry, rub the flour, sugar, and butter together by hand, or in a food processor, until the mixture resembles fine breadcrumbs. Add the egg yolk and bring the mixture together to form a soft dough. Add a little more water if needed. Wrap and chill for 30 minutes. Preheat the oven to 180°C (350°F/Gas 4).

**2** Roll out the pastry on a floured surface to 3mm (⅛in) thick and use to line a 23cm (9in) loose-bottomed tart tin, leaving an overhang of at least 1cm (½in). Trim off any excess pastry that hangs down further than this. Prick the bottom with a fork, brush with the egg white to seal, line the pastry case with a piece of silicone or greaseproof paper, and fill with baking beans. Place the case on a baking tray and bake for 20 minutes. Remove the beans and paper, and bake for a further 5 minutes, if the centre looks uncooked. Trim off any ragged edges from the pastry case while still warm.

**3** For the filling, whisk the cream, sugar, eggs, egg yolk, and vanilla together in a large bowl. Lay the apricots, face down, evenly over the bottom of the cooked tart case. Place the tart case on a baking tray and pour the cream mixture carefully over the fruit. Bake for 30–35 minutes until lightly golden and just set. Set the tart aside to cool to room temperature before dusting with icing sugar and serving with fresh cream.

**SERVES** 6-8     **PREP** 30 MINS, PLUS CHILLING **COOK** 50 MINS–1 HOUR

Here, the sweetness of the ripe blueberries is balanced by a tangy mix of soured cream and cream cheese. The perfect end to a dinner party, serve this tart with thick cream or a berry compote.

# Blueberry cream cheese tart

**For the pastry**
175g (6oz) plain flour,
   plus extra for dusting
85g (3oz) butter, diced
2 tbsp caster sugar
1 egg yolk

**For the filling**
115g (4oz) cream cheese
60g (2oz) soured cream
60g (2oz) caster sugar
a pinch of grated nutmeg
3 eggs, beaten
zest of 1 lemon
350g (12oz) blueberries
icing sugar, for dusting

**1** To make the pastry, rub the flour and butter together with your fingertips, or pulse in a food processor, until the mixture resembles breadcrumbs. Stir in the sugar, add the egg yolk, and mix to form a firm dough. Roll out the pastry on a lightly floured surface and use to line a 23cm (9in) loose-bottomed tart tin. Prick the bottom with a fork. Wrap in cling film and chill for 30 minutes. Preheat the oven to 200°C (400°F/Gas 6).

**2** Line the pastry case with greaseproof paper and fill with baking beans. Bake for 10 minutes, then remove the paper and beans, and bake for a further 10 minutes, or until pale golden. Remove from the oven, and reduce the heat to 180°C (350°F/Gas 4).

**3** To make the filling, beat together the cream cheese, soured cream, sugar, nutmeg, eggs, and lemon zest until well combined. Pour into the pastry case and scatter the blueberries over the surface. Bake for 25–30 minutes until just set. Set aside to cool before transferring to a serving plate. Serve warm or cold, dusted with icing sugar. The tart case can be made several days in advance and kept in the refrigerator.

**SERVES** 8    **PREP** 25 MINS, PLUS CHILLING **COOK** 45-50 MINS

Here brown sugar and cinnamon add a sweet, dark spicy flavour to the plum filling. A cobbler topping can be used to cover any frui suitable for cooking, making it a year-round favourite.

# Plum and cinnamon cobbler

**For the filling**
1kg (2¼lb) plums, stoned and halved
50g (1¾oz) soft light brown sugar
1 tsp ground cinnamon
25g (scant 1oz) unsalted butter,
   chilled and diced

**For the cobbler topping**
225g (8oz) self-raising flour
2 tsp baking powder
75g (2½oz) caster sugar
a pinch of salt
½–¾ tsp ground cinnamon, to taste
75g (2½oz) unsalted butter
1 egg
100ml (3fl oz) buttermilk
1 tbsp soft light brown sugar

**1** Preheat the oven to 190°C (375°F/Gas 5). For the filling, toss plums with the sugar and ground cinnamon. Put them in an ovenproof dish and dot with the diced butter.

**2** To make the cobbler topping, sift the flour, baking powder, caster sugar, salt, and cinnamon into a bowl. Rub in the butter until the mixture resembles fine breadcrumbs. Whisk together the egg and buttermilk, then add the liquid to the dry ingredients, and bring it together to form a soft, sticky dough.

**3** Drop heaped tablespoons of the dough over the surface of the fruit, leaving a little space between them. Sprinkle with the soft light brown sugar.

**4** Bake for 30 minutes, or until golden and bubbling. The cobbler is ready when a skewer inserted into the centre of the topping comes out clean. Set aside to cool, for at least 5 minutes, before serving with ice cream, custard, or cream.

**SERVES** 6-8   **PREP** 20 MINS **COOK** 30 MINS

This perennial favourite never fails to delight family and friends. Make double or triple quantity of the crumble topping and store it in a plastic food bag in the freezer for last-minute puddings.

# Plum crumble

**For the crumble topping**
150g (5½oz) plain flour
100g (3½oz) butter, chilled and diced
75g (2½oz) light soft brown sugar
60g (2oz) rolled oats

**For the filling**
600g (1lb 5oz) plums, stoned and halved
maple syrup or honey, to drizzle

**1** Preheat the oven to 200°C (400°F/Gas 6). To make the crumble topping, place the flour in a large bowl and rub in the butter with your fingertips until the mixture resembles breadcrumbs. Do not make the breadcrumbs too fine or your crumble will have a stodgy top. Stir in the sugar and oats.

**2** Place the plums in an ovenproof dish, drizzle the maple syrup or honey over, and top with the crumble mixture. Bake for 30–40 minutes until the top is golden brown and the plum juices are bubbling. Serve hot. The crumble mixture can be made 1 month in advance and stored in the freezer until ready to use.

**SERVES** 4    **PREP** 10 MINS **COOK** 30-40 MINS    **FREEZE** UP TO 2 MONTHS

The classic American cherry pie is given a delicate, decorative lattice topping, making it just the thing to serve after a summer dinner party. Best served warm with vanilla ice cream.

# Cherry lattice pie

**For the pastry**
250g (9oz) plain flour,
  plus extra for dusting
1 tsp salt
125g (4½oz) lard or white
  vegetable fat, chilled and diced
75g (2½oz) unsalted butter,
  chilled and diced
1 egg, to glaze

**For the filling**
500g (1lb 2oz) cherries, stoned
200g (7oz) caster sugar
45g (1½oz) plain flour
¼ tsp almond extract (optional)

**1** To make the pastry, sift the flour and ½ tsp salt into a bowl. Rub the lard and butter into the flour with your fingertips until the mixture resembles breadcrumbs. Sprinkle with 3 tbsp water, and mix until the dough forms a ball. Wrap in cling film and chill for 30 minutes.

**2** Preheat the oven to 200°C (400°F/Gas 6). Roll out two-thirds of the pastry on a lightly floured surface and use to line a 23cm (9in) loose-bottomed pie tin, with some pastry hanging over the edge. Press pastry into the dish and chill for 15 minutes.

**3** For the filling, place the cherries in a bowl and add the sugar, flour, and almond extract if using. Stir until well mixed, then spoon into the pastry-lined tin.

**4** Roll out the remaining pastry into a rectangle. Cut out 8 strips, each 1cm (½in) wide, and arrange them in a lattice-like pattern on top of the pie, then trim the pastry. Beat the egg with ½ teaspoon of salt, and use this to glaze the pastry lattice. Secure the strips to the edge of the pie. Bake for 40–45 minutes until the pastry is golden brown. Serve at room temperature or chilled. The pie can be kept in an airtight container for 2 days, but is best eaten on the day it is baked.

**SERVES** 8    **PREP** 40-45 MINS, PLUS CHILLING **COOK** 40-45 MINS    **FREEZE** UP TO 1 MONTH

These delicious, little, fried pastries are found all over Brazil, stuffed with both sweet and savoury fillings. A small amount of alcohol is used in the pastry, which could be omitted, if preferred.

# Banana and cinnamon pastels

**For the pastry**
300g (10oz) plain flour,
   plus extra for dusting
½ tsp salt
2 tbsp sunflower oil
1 tbsp Cachaça or vodka
1 tbsp white vinegar

**For the filling**
1 large banana
2 tbsp muscovado sugar
1 tsp ground cinnamon
vegetable oil, for deep frying
icing sugar, for dusting

**1** To make the pastry, mix the flour and salt in a bowl. Stir in the sunflower oil, Cachaça, and vinegar. Then gradually add 120ml (4fl oz) warm water, stirring well to form a smooth dough. On a well-floured surface, knead the dough very lightly. Wrap in cling film and chill for 1 hour.

**2** For the filling, mash the banana in a small dish and stir in the sugar and cinnamon.

**3** Divide the dough into 2 equal pieces. On a well-floured surface, roll out one piece of the dough to form a rectangle 18 x 30cm (7 x 12in). Cut the dough into 5 rectangles measuring 6 x 18cm (2½ x 7in) each. Put a little filling on one half of each rectangle, brush the edges with water, fold, and press firmly together, to seal, using the tines of a fork. Repeat to use up the remaining dough and filling.

**4** Heat the vegetable oil in a deep pan to 180°C (350°F). Fry the pastels, 2 at a time, for about 1½–2 minutes until golden brown. Transfer the cooked pastels to a plate lined with kitchen paper, to drain. Serve hot, dusted with icing sugar.

**SERVES** 10     **PREP** 35 MINS, PLUS CHILLING **COOK** 10 MINS

Using a good-quality, shop-bought crust is a great time saver for this truly decadent dessert. Use ripe fresh raspberries and the best quality white and dark chocolate that you can find.

# Double chocolate raspberry tart

**For the filling**
100g (3½oz) good-quality white
 chocolate, broken into pieces
75g (2½oz) good-quality dark
 chocolate, broken into pieces
250ml (9fl oz) double cream
400g (14oz) raspberries
icing sugar, for dusting

**For the pastry**
ready-made chocolate pastry case
 (or make your own, see p328)

**1** Melt the white chocolate in a heatproof bowl, set over a saucepan of barely simmering water. Set the chocolate aside to cool.

**2** Melt the dark chocolate in the same way, then use a pastry brush to paint the inside of the tart case with a layer of the chocolate. This will stop the pastry case going soggy once it is filled with the creamy filling. Set the pastry case aside until the chocolate has set.

**3** Whip the cream stiffly. Fold the cooled white chocolate into the whipped cream. Crush half the raspberries and fold them through the cream mixture. Pile the filling into the pastry case evenly. Decorate with the remaining raspberries, dust with icing sugar, and serve. The tart will keep in an airtight container in the refrigerator for 2 days.

**SERVES** 6–8　　**PREP** 20 MINS, PLUS COOLING **COOK** 5–10 MINS

Fresh raspberries and dark chocolate are a classic combination
and here they combine to make the ultimate in luxurious desserts

# Raspberry tart with chocolate cream

**For the pastry**
130g (4½oz) plain flour,
    plus extra for dusting
20g (¾oz) cocoa powder
100g (3½oz) unsalted butter,
    chilled and diced
50g (1¾oz) caster sugar
1 egg yolk
½ tsp vanilla extract

**For the filling**
100g (3½oz) caster sugar
50g (1¾oz) cornflour, sifted
2 eggs
1 tsp vanilla extract
450ml (15fl oz) whole milk
175g (6oz) good-quality dark
    chocolate, broken into pieces
400g (14oz) raspberries
icing sugar, for dusting

**1** To make the pastry, rub the flour, cocoa, and butter together with your fingertips until they resemble fine breadcrumbs. Stir in the sugar. Beat the egg yolk with the vanilla and add to the flour mixture, bringing it together to form a soft dough. Add a little water if it seems too stiff. Wrap in cling film and chill for 30 minutes.

**2** Preheat the oven to 180°C (350°F/Gas 4). Roll out pastry on a floured surface to 3mm (⅛in) thick. Use to line a 23cm (9in) loose-bottomed tart tin, leaving an overlapping edge of 2cm (¾in). Prick bottom with a fork, then line with baking parchment and fill with baking beans. Bake for 20 minutes. Remove beans and paper, and bake for a further 5 minutes. Trim excess pastry.

**3** For the filling, beat together the sugar, cornflour, eggs, and vanilla. Put the milk and 100g (3½oz) chocolate in a pan and bring to the boil, whisking constantly. Pour onto egg mixture, whisking constantly. Return to cleaned pan and bring to the boil, whisking. When it thickens, reduce heat to its lowest and cook for 2–3 minutes, whisking. Turn into a bowl, cover, and cool.

**4** Melt remaining chocolate in a bowl set over a pan of simmering water, and brush inside of tart case. Leave to set. Beat the cooled filling with a wooden spoon, and spread over the case. Arrange the raspberries on top, remove tart from the tin, and serve dusted with icing sugar. .

**SERVES** 6–8    **PREP** 40 MINS, PLUS CHILLING **COOK** 20-25 MINS    **FREEZE** UP TO 3 MONTHS, PASTRY CASE

For a perfect result, chill the bottom two layers until they firm up, but remove the pie from the refrigerator 30 minutes before serving, and top with the bananas and cream at the last minute.

# Banoffee pie

**For the biscuit case**
250g (9oz) digestive biscuits
100g (3½oz) unsalted butter,
  melted and cooled

**For the caramel**
50g (1¾oz) unsalted butter
50g (1¾oz) soft light brown sugar
400g can condensed milk

**For the topping**
2 large, ripe bananas
250ml (9fl oz) double cream, whipped
a little dark chocolate, to decorate

**1** Line a 23cm (9in) springform cake tin or loose-bottomed tart tin with baking parchment. To make the biscuit case, put the biscuits into a sturdy plastic bag, and use a rolling pin to crush them finely. Mix crushed biscuits with the melted butter, and tip them into the prepared tin. Press them down firmly to create a compressed, even layer. Cover and chill.

**2** To make the caramel, melt the butter and sugar in a small, heavy saucepan over a medium heat. Add the condensed milk and bring to the boil. Reduce the heat and simmer for 2–3 minutes, stirring constantly. It will thicken and take on a light caramel colour. Pour the caramel over the crushed biscuit case and leave to set.

**3** Once set, remove the biscuit and caramel case from the tin and transfer to a serving plate. Peel and slice the bananas thinly into 5mm (¼in) discs, cut slightly on a diagonal, and use them to cover the surface of the caramel.

**4** Spread the cream over the bananas using a spatula until smooth, then decorate with finely grated chocolate and larger chocolate curls, made by grating the chocolate with a vegetable peeler. The pie will keep in an airtight container in the refrigerator for 2 days.

**SERVES** 6–8    **PREP** 20 MINS, PLUS CHILLING **COOK** 5-10 MINS    **FREEZE** UP TO 2 MONTHS

These unusual little tartlets have to be tasted to be believed and will be a hit with adults and children alike. Serve with cream.

# Banana and Nutella crumble tartlets

**For the pastry**
175g (6oz) plain flour, plus
    extra for dusting
25g (scant 1oz) caster sugar
100g (3½oz) unsalted
    butter, softened
1 egg yolk, beaten with
    2 tbsp cold water

**For the filling**
25g (scant 1oz) plain flour
25g (scant 1oz) soft light
    brown sugar
10g (¼oz) desiccated coconut
25g (scant 1oz) butter, softened
2–3 bananas, not too ripe
4 tbsp Nutella

**1** To make the pastry, rub the flour, caster sugar, and butter together, by hand or in a food processor, until they resemble fine breadcrumbs. Add the egg yolk and bring the mixture together to form a soft dough; add a little water if needed. Wrap and chill for 30 minutes.

**2** Preheat the oven to 180°C (350°F/Gas 4). Roll out pastry on a floured surface to 3mm (⅛in) thick and use to line 6 x 10cm (4in) tart tins, leaving overhanging edge of 1cm (½in). Prick with a fork, line with greaseproof paper, and fill with baking beans. Place on a baking tray and bake for 15 minutes. Remove beans and paper and return to the oven for 5 minutes. Trim off any ragged edges while still warm. Turn oven up to 200°C (400°F/Gas 6).

**3** For the filling, mix together the flour, sugar, and coconut in a bowl. Rub in the butter, making sure the mixture isn't too well mixed, and that some lumps of butter remain.

**4** Peel and slice bananas into 1cm (½in) slices on a diagonal slant, and arrange on the bottom of the tart cases, breaking them to fit if needed. Spread 1 tbsp Nutella over banana to cover. Divide the crumble mix between the tarts and loosely spread it over, taking care not to pack it down. Bake for 15 minutes until the crumble has started to brown.

**SERVES** 6    **PREP** 20 MINS, PLUS CHILLING **COOK** 35 MINS    **FREEZE** UP TO 2 MONTHS, PASTRY CASE

Iranian nibbed pistachios are the best type of nuts to use for this tart, as they give a vivid, bright green colour to the finished dish.

# Pistachio and orange flower tart

**For the pastry**
175g (6oz) plain flour,
  plus extra for dusting
25g (scant 1oz) caster sugar
100g (3½oz) unsalted butter, softened
1 egg yolk, beaten with
  2 tbsp cold water

**For the filling**
75g (2½oz) unsalted butter
200g (7oz) nibbed pistachios
4 eggs
100g (3½oz) caster sugar
½ tbsp orange flower water
2 tbsp runny honey
icing sugar, for dusting

**1** To make the pastry, rub flour, sugar, and butter together with your fingertips until the mixture resembles fine breadcrumbs. Add egg yolk and bring mixture together to form a soft dough. If the dough is too dry, add a little water. Wrap and chill for 30 minutes.

**2** Preheat the oven to 180°C (350°F/Gas 4). Roll out pastry on a floured surface to 3mm (⅛in) thick and use to line a 23cm (9in) loose-bottomed tart tin, leaving an overlapping edge of at least 1cm (½in). Prick with a fork, line with greaseproof paper, and fill with baking beans. Place on a baking tray and bake for 20 minutes. Remove beans and paper, and return to the oven for a further 5 minutes. Trim off any ragged edges while still warm.

**3** To make the filling, first melt the butter and set aside to cool. Next, finely grind the pistachios in a food processor. Whisk together the eggs, sugar, orange flower water, and honey. Whisk in the cooled, melted butter, then fold in the ground pistachios. Place tart case on a baking tray and carefully pour the filling in. Bake immediately (or filling may separate) for 25–30 minutes until the centre has just set.

**4** Set tart aside to cool for 15 minutes, then dust with icing sugar and serve warm, or at room temperature, with whipped cream flavoured with a little orange flower water. Best eaten on the day it is made.

**SERVES** 6-8   **PREP** 30 MINS, PLUS CHILLING AND COOLING   **FREEZE** UP TO 3 MONTHS,
**COOK** 50-55 MINS   PASTRY CASE

Rich, buttery shortcrust tartlets can be baked in bulk and frozen for future use. Just crisp them up in a hot oven for a few minutes before filling, here with a deliciously thick coconut cream.

# Coconut cream tartlets

**For the pastry**
150g (5½oz) plain flour,
    plus extra for dusting
100g (3½oz) unsalted butter, diced,
    plus extra for greasing
50g (1¾oz) caster sugar
1 egg yolk
½ tsp vanilla extract

**For the filling**
400ml tin coconut milk
240ml (8½fl oz) whole milk
4 egg yolks
50g (1¾oz) caster sugar
4 tbsp cornflour
1 tsp vanilla extract
4 tbsp desiccated coconut

**1** Preheat the oven to 200°C (400°F/Gas 6). Lightly grease 4 x 12cm (5in) tart tins. To make the pastry, rub flour and butter together in a bowl with your fingertips until the mixture resembles breadcrumbs. Stir in sugar. Add the egg yolk and vanilla and bring together to form a smooth dough, adding 1–2 tbsp cold water if needed. Wrap and chill for 30 minutes.

**2** For the filling, heat coconut milk and whole milk in a pan, until just boiling. Whisk egg yolks, sugar, cornflour, and vanilla together in a heatproof bowl. Gradually pour in the hot milk, whisking constantly. Return mixture to the pan and stir over a medium heat until it thickens. Remove from heat, cover with greaseproof paper, and leave to cool.

**3** Divide pastry equally into 4 parts. Roll out one piece on a well-floured surface to a circle large enough to line one of the tins. Place the pastry in the tin and trim the edges. Prick with a fork and place on a baking tray. Repeat with remaining pastry. Chill for 30 minutes.

**4** Line each tartlet case with foil, pressing it down well. Bake for 5 minutes, then remove the foil, and bake for a further 5 minutes. Set aside to cool.

**5** In a small, dry frying pan, lightly toast the coconut over a medium heat, shaking the pan occasionally. Remove pastry cases from the tins. An hour before serving, spoon the cooled coconut custard into the pastry cases and chill for 1 hour. Sprinkle with the toasted coconut to serve.

**SERVES** 4     **PREP** 30 MINS, PLUS CHILLING **COOK** 20 MINS

Otherwise known as "Grandmother's Tart", this classic Italian recipe is made using the freshest of ricotta and little else. This tart is fantastic served still warm from the oven drizzled with honey.

# Torta della nonna

**For the pastry**
150g (5½oz) plain flour,
    plus extra for dusting
100g (3½oz) unsalted butter, cubed
50g (1¾oz) caster sugar
1 egg yolk
½ tsp vanilla extract

**For the filling**
400g (14oz) ricotta cheese
2 large eggs
zest and juice of 1 lemon
75g (2½oz) icing sugar, sifted,
    plus extra for dusting
1 tsp almond extract
70g (1¼oz) toasted pine nuts
30g (1oz) toasted sliced almonds

**1** To make the pastry, rub the flour and butter together in a bowl with your fingertips until the mixture resembles breadcrumbs. Stir in the sugar. Add the egg yolk and vanilla and bring together to form a smooth dough, adding 1–2 tsp cold water if needed. Wrap and chill for 30 minutes.

**2** For the filling, place ricotta and eggs in a large bowl and whisk until smooth. Stir in the lemon zest and juice, icing sugar, and almond extract. Set aside. Preheat the oven to 180°C (350°F/Gas 4).

**3** Roll out the pastry on a floured surface to a circle large enough to line a lightly greased 20cm (8in) loose-bottomed deep tart tin. Place pastry in tin, pressing it down well into the bottom and around the edges. Trim off any excess pastry, prick the bottom with a fork, and line with baking parchment. Place tin on a baking tray and fill with baking beans. Bake for 20 minutes. Remove the beans and paper and bake for a further 5–10 minutes to crisp.

**4** Evenly scatter the pine nuts over the pastry base. Spoon the cheese mixture in, spread it out in an even layer, and sprinkle the almonds over the top. Bake tart for 30–35 minutes until the filling is just set. Transfer to a wire rack and set aside to cool for 15 minutes. Serve dusted with icing sugar.

**SERVES** 6    **PREP** 20 MINS, PLUS CHILLING **COOK** 1 HOUR 5 MINS    **FREEZE** UP TO 1 MONTH, PASTRY CASE

Originating from the southern United States where pecans are widely grown, a little of this traditional pie goes a very long way.

# Pecan pie

**For the pastry**
150g (5½oz) plain flour,
    plus extra for dusting
100g (3½oz) unsalted butter,
    chilled and diced
50g (1¾oz) caster sugar
1 egg yolk
½ tsp vanilla extract

**For the filling**
150ml (5fl oz) maple syrup
60g (2oz) butter
175g (6oz) soft light brown sugar
a few drops of vanilla extract
pinch of salt
3 eggs
200g (7oz) pecan nuts

**1** To make the pastry, rub flour and butter together with your fingertips until the mixture resembles fine breadcrumbs. Stir in the sugar. Beat the egg yolk with the vanilla extract and mix into the dry ingredients, bringing the mixture together to form a soft dough; add a little water to bring the dough together, if necessary. Wrap and chill in the refrigerator for 30 minutes.

**2** Preheat the oven to 180°C (350°F/Gas 4). Roll out pastry on a well-floured surface to 3mm (⅛in) thick and use it to line a 23cm (9in) loose-bottomed tart tin, leaving an overlapping edge of at least 2cm (¾in). Prick the bottom with a fork, line with baking parchment, and fill with baking beans. Place on a baking sheet and bake for 20 minutes. Remove beans and paper, and bake for a further 5 minutes, if the centre looks uncooked.

**3** To make the filling, pour the maple syrup into a pan, and add the butter, sugar, vanilla extract, and salt. Place pan over a low heat and stir constantly until the butter has melted and the sugar dissolved. Set the mixture aside to cool until it feels just tepid, then beat in the eggs, one at a time. Stir in pecans, then pour mixture into pastry case.

**4** Bake for 40–50 minutes until just set. Cover with foil if it is browning too quickly. Transfer pie to a wire rack, and set aside to cool for 15–20 minutes. Remove pie from the tin and serve warm or leave it on the wire rack to cool completely.

**SERVES** 6–8　**PREP** 15 MINS, PLUS CHILLING **COOK** 1½ HOURS　**FREEZE** UP TO 3 MONTHS, PASTRY CASE

A rich, dark chocolate tart such as this one is a wonderful way to finish a meal, but remember, a little goes a long way. Best served just-set and still warm from the oven, with thick, cold cream.

# Chocolate tart

**For the pastry**
150g (5½oz) plain flour,
   plus extra for dusting
100g (3½oz) butter, chilled and diced
50g (1¾oz) caster sugar
1 egg yolk
½ tsp vanilla extract

**For the filling**
150g (5½oz) unsalted butter, diced
200g (7oz) dark chocolate, chopped
3 eggs
30g (1oz) caster sugar
100ml (3½fl oz) double cream

**1** For the pastry, rub the flour and butter together in a large bowl with your fingertips until the mixture resembles breadcrumbs. Stir in the sugar. Beat the egg yolk and vanilla, add to the bowl, and bring mixture together to form a dough; add 1–2 tsps cold water if too dry. Wrap and chill in the refrigerator for 30 minutes. Preheat the oven to 180°C (350°F/Gas 4).

**2** Roll out the pastry on a floured surface to 3mm (⅛in) thick and use to line a 22cm (9in) loose-bottomed tart tin, leaving an overlapping edge of 2cm (¾in). Trim off any excess pastry. Prick the bottom with a fork, line with baking parchment, and fill with baking beans. Place on a baking tray and bake for 20 minutes. Remove beans and paper and return to the oven for another 5 minutes. Trim off excess pastry and set aside.

**3** To make the filling, melt butter and chocolate in a bowl, set over a pan of simmering water. Let cool. Whisk eggs and sugar together in another bowl, then stir in the cooled chocolate mixture. Mix in the cream. Put the pastry case, still in the tin, on a baking tray and pour in the filling. Bake for 10–15 minutes until just set. Cool for 5 minutes and serve.

**SERVES** 8–10     **PREP** 30 MINS, PLUS CHILLING **COOK** 35-40 MINS     **FREEZE** UP TO 3 MONTHS
PASTRY CASE

This recipe will have your children begging for more, and most likely the adults too. This delicious pie is best if it is served still warm, with vanilla ice cream or a spoonful of whipped cream.

# Chocolate chip cookie pie

**For the pastry**
150g (5½oz) plain flour,
  plus extra for dusting
100g (3½oz) unsalted butter
50g (1¾oz) caster sugar
1 egg yolk

**For the filling**
2 eggs
50g (1¾oz) plain flour
75g (2½oz) caster sugar
75g (2½oz) dark soft brown sugar
125g (4½oz) butter, chilled and cubed
50g (1¾oz) milk chocolate chips
50g (1¾oz) white chocolate chips

**1** To make the pastry, rub flour and butter together in a bowl with your fingertips until the mixture resembles fine breadcrumbs. Stir in the sugar. Add the egg yolk and bring the mixture together to form a smooth dough, adding 1–2 tsps cold water if needed. Wrap in cling film and chill in the refrigerator for 30 minutes.

**2** Preheat the oven to 180°C (350°F/Gas 4). Roll out the pastry on a floured surface to a circle large enough to line a deep 20cm (8in) loose-bottomed tart tin. Place pastry in the tin, pressing down well into the bottom and around the edges. Trim off any excess pastry, prick the bottom with a fork, and line with baking parchment. Place tin on a baking tray and fill with baking beans. Bake for 20 minutes. Remove beans and paper and bake for a further 5 minutes. Reduce the oven temperature to 160°C (325°F/Gas 3).

**3** For the filling, place the eggs in a large bowl and, using an electric whisk, whisk for 2–3 minutes, or until they are foamy. Whisk in the flour and sugars. Add the butter and whisk until the mixture is smooth.

**4** Sprinkle the chocolate chips over the bottom of the pastry case and spoon the filling over, in an even layer. Bake for 50–55 minutes until the filling is set. Set aside to cool on a wire rack.

**SERVES** 6     **PREP** 20 MINS, PLUS CHILLING
**COOK** 1½-1 HOURS 20 MINS     **FREEZE** UP TO 1 MONTH, PASTRY CASE

This pie heralds from the Pennsylvania region of the USA. It uses a lot of molasses, and supposedly got its name from the fact that it was so sweet, you had to "shoo" the flies from gathering around it

# Shoo fly pie

**For the pastry**
175g (6oz) plain flour, plus extra for dusting
25g (scant 1oz) caster sugar
100g (3½oz) unsalted butter, at room temperature, cut into pieces
1 egg yolk, beaten with 2 tbsp cold water

**For the filling**
150g (5½oz) plain flour
100g (3½oz) soft light brown sugar
1 tsp mixed spice
50g (1¾oz) unsalted butter, softened
150g (5½oz) molasses or black treacle
½ tsp bicarbonate of soda
1 egg

**1** To make the pastry, rub the flour, sugar, and butter together with your fingertips until the mixture resembles fine breadcrumbs. Add the egg yolk and bring the mixture together to form a soft dough; add a little water if needed. Wrap and chill for 30 minutes.

**2** Preheat the oven to 180°C (350°F/Gas 4). Roll out the pastry on a floured surface to 3mm (⅛in) thick and use to line a 23cm (9in) loose-bottomed tart tin, leaving an overlapping edge of at least 1cm (½in). Trim off any excess pastry. Prick the bottom with a fork, line with greaseproof paper, and fill with baking beans. Place on a baking tray and bake for 20 minutes. Remove beans and paper, and bake for a further 5 minutes if the centre looks a little uncooked. Trim any ragged edges from the pastry case while it is still warm, and set aside. Turn oven heat up to 190°C (375°F/Gas 5).

**3** For the filling, mix the flour, sugar, and mixed spice together in a bowl. Rub in the butter until the mixture resembles fine breadcrumbs, and set aside. Put the molasses or black treacle in another bowl. Mix 100ml (3½fl oz) boiling water with the bicarbonate of soda and whisk it into the molasses until dissolved. Set aside to cool.

**4** Whisk the egg into the cooled molasses mixture. Set aside 4 heaped tbsp crumb mixture, and whisk the rest into the molasses. Pour the filling into the tart case. Scatter the remaining crumbs over the top and bake for 30 minutes until pie is puffed up and just set. Serve warm or at room temperature with thick cream or vanilla ice cream.

**SERVES** 6–8    **PREP** 20 MINS, PLUS CHILLING AND COOLING **COOK** 50-55 MINS    **FREEZE** UP TO 3 MONTHS, PASTRY CASE

An ice-cream pie is the perfect dessert to serve in hot weather. Use good-quality chocolate ice cream and your favourite types of nuts for the ultimate sweet treat.

# Rocky road ice-cream pie

**For the biscuit case**
250g (9oz) digestive or Breton biscuits
60g (2oz) caster sugar
125g (4½oz) unsalted butter,
    melted and cooled

**For the filling**
1 litre good quality chocolate ice cream
30g (1oz) mini marshmallows
50g (1¾oz) pecans, roughly chopped
50g (1¾oz) blanched almonds,
    roughly chopped

**1** Preheat the oven to 180°C (350°F/Gas 4). To make the biscuit case, crush the biscuits by hand, or in a food processor until they resemble fine breadcrumbs. Mix biscuit crumbs with the sugar and melted butter until the mixture resembles wet sand.

**2** Pour the biscuit mixture into a 23cm 9(in) loose-bottomed tart tin, and press it firmly into the bottom and sides of the tin. Make sure the mixture is as packed as possible, and that there is a good side to the case (it should go at least 3cm/1¼in up the sides of the tin). Bake the tart case for 10 minutes, then set aside to cool. Once cold, store the tart case in the refrigerator until needed.

**3** For the filling, take the ice cream out of the freezer at least 15 minutes before needed, to allow it to soften in the refrigerator. Scoop the ice cream into a food processor with a large spoon. Don't just tip the whole block in, as it will be too difficult to break down quickly. Process the ice cream until it is thick and creamy, but entirely smooth. Quickly scrape it into a large bowl, and fold in the mini marshmallows and chopped nuts. Pour the mixture into the prepared case and freeze for 1 hour, or until firm. Remove pie from the freezer and leave in the refrigerator for about 20–30 minutes to soften before serving.

**SERVES** 8      **PREP** 20 MINS, PLUS CHILLING AND COOLING      **FREEZE** UP TO 2 MONTHS
        **COOK** 10 MINS

Pear and ginger is a fabulous combination, and using a mixture of ginger biscuits, stem ginger, and ginger syrup adds layers of flavour to this classic pie. Make sure the ice cream is soft enough to scoop

# Pear and ginger ice-cream pie

**For the biscuit base**
75g (2½oz) unsalted butter
  plus extra for greasing
250g (9oz) ginger biscuits, crushed

**For the topping**
1 litre tub good-quality vanilla ice cream
5 pieces stem ginger preserved
  in syrup, drained
2 tbsp stem ginger syrup,
  plus extra for drizzling
415g can pear halves in natural juice,
  drained and finely chopped

**1** Grease and line the bottom of a 23cm (9in) springform cake tin with baking parchment. Take the ice cream out of the freezer to allow it to soften.

**2** To make the biscuit base, melt the butter in a saucepan and mix in the crushed biscuits. Turn the mixture into the prepared tin and press down with the back of a metal tablespoon.

**3** For the topping, scoop the softened ice cream, stem ginger pieces, and stem ginger syrup into a food processor. Process until the ice cream is thick and creamy, but smooth. Pour into a bowl and stir in the chopped pears. Pour the mixture onto the biscuit base in the tin and freeze the pie for at least 2 hours, until completely frozen.

**4** To serve the ice-cream pie, remove it from the freezer and place it on a serving plate in the refrigerator for 30 minutes, then unclip the tin and remove the sides. Drizzle a little ginger syrup over the top and slice to serve.

**SERVES** 8 **PREP** 20 MINS, PLUS FREEZING **COOK** 5-10 MINS **FREEZE** UP TO 1 MONTH

A family favourite, the flavours of this pie are simply made to be together – sharp lemon and sweet vanilla meringue.

# Lemon meringue pie

**For the pastry**
butter, for greasing
400g (14oz) ready-made sweet shortcrust
   pastry (or to make your own see p229)
flour, for dusting

**For the filling**
6 eggs, at room temperature, separated
3 tbsp cornflour
3 tbsp plain flour
400g (14oz) caster sugar
juice of 3 lemons
1 tbsp finely grated lemon zest
45g (1½oz) butter, diced
½ tsp cream of tartar
½ tsp vanilla extract

**1** Preheat the oven to 200°C (400°F/Gas 6). Roll out pastry on a floured surface and use to line a greased 23cm (9in) loose-bottomed tart tin. Line with baking parchment, fill with baking beans, and bake for 10–15 minutes until just golden. Remove paper and beans and bake for 3–5 minutes more. Set aside. Reduce oven to 180°C (350°F/Gas 4).

**2** For the filling, lightly beat the egg yolks. Combine cornflour, flour, and 225g (8oz) sugar in a pan. Slowly add 360ml (12fl oz) water and heat gently, stirring, until sugar dissolves. Increase the heat slightly and cook, stirring, until the mixture starts to thicken.

**3** Beat several spoonfuls of the hot mixture into the yolks. Pour back into the pan and slowly bring to the boil, stirring. Boil for 3 minutes, then stir in lemon juice, zest, and butter. Boil for a further 2 minutes until the mixtue is thick and glossy, stirring and scraping down the sides of the pan as necessary. Remove from the heat and cover.

**4** To make the meringue, whisk egg whites in a clean bowl until foamy. Whisk in cream of tartar., then whisk in remaining sugar, 1 tbsp at a time. Add the vanilla with the last spoon of sugar, whisking until thick and glossy.

**5** Pour filling into the pastry case, then spread the meringue over the top to cover filling. Bake for 12–15 minutes until meringue is golden. Cool on a wire rack before serving.

**SERVES** 8 **PREP** 30 MINS **COOK** 40-50 MINS

# Index

# Acknowledgments

Dorling Kindersley would like to thank:
**Art directors for photoshoots:** Nicky Collings, Katherine Mead, Luis Peral, Sara Robin, Kathryn Wilding
**Food stylists:** Katie Giovanni, Jane Lawrie, Rosie Reynolds, Annie Rigg, Bridget Sargeson
**Props stylists:** Rob Merret, Sue Rowlands, Wei Tang
**Recipe testers:** Jane Bamforth, Rebecca Blackstone, Anna Burges-Lumsden, Louisa Carter, Sonja Edridge, Jan Fullwood, Laura Fyfe, Katy Greenwood, Anne Harnan, Richard Harris, Lisa Harrison, Sylvain Jamois, Emma Lahaye, Ann Reynolds, Natalie Seldon, Rachel Wood

**Picture Credits**
All images © Dorling Kindersley
For further information see: www.dkimages.com